JIMMY GREAVES AT SEVENTY
TERRY BAKER
Michael Giller
Edited by Norman Giller
Introduced by JIMMY GREAVES

NMG

A NormanMichaelGillerEnterprises publication
in association with Terry Baker, of A1 Sporting Speakers
© Terry Baker/Norman Giller/Michael Giller 2010

First published in 2010 by NMG Enterprises
PO Box 3386, Ferndown, BH22 8XT

A CIP catalogue for this title is available from the British Library
ISBN 978-0-9543243-5-3

Typeset and designed by NMG Enterprises, Dorset, UK
Printed and bound in the United Kingdom by CPI Antony Rowe
Bumper's Farm, Chippenham, Wiltshire SN14 6LH

The majority of photographs in this book have been provided by premier promotions agency
A1 Sporting Speakers (www.a1sportingspeakers.com). There are also photos from the private
collections of Jimmy Greaves, Dave Mackay, Terry Baker, NMG Publishing and various photo
agencies and Tottenham supporters. Best efforts have been made to clear all copyrights. The
head-and-shoulders drawing of Greavsie running through the book is by illustrator Art Turner.

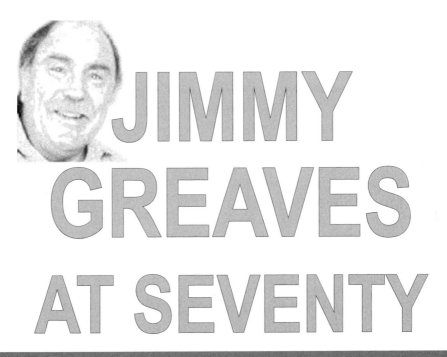

JIMMY GREAVES
AT SEVENTY

The official, authorised and most complete biography

TERRY BAKER
Michael Giller

Edited by Norman Giller

Introduced by
Jimmy Greaves

NMG

Dedicated to my pal, my hero Jimmy Greaves, who invited me to No 10 Downing Street to see him – at long last – receive his 1966 World Cup medal

Also for Freda, Jackson, Nicole, Shelley, Maria, Tara, Mum, my friends everywhere and to Irene. My love to you all.

With sincere thanks to Norman and Michael Giller for all your help, Chris Jinks, Marie, Dave O and Phil and Debbie for your hard work, Mike from the hugely informative and entertaining Backpass magazine. And finally to anyone who has been to our shows or bought our memorabilia, thanks for supporting me and Jimmy.

See where we are on www.jimmygreaves.net or feel free to email me for booking enquiries terry@a1sportingspeakers.com

JIMMY GREAVES AT SEVENTY: *Contents*

Jimmy and Irene, living and loving together for more than 50 years

THIS is the first time I've ever been seventy, and I can't quite get my head around it. Wasn't it just the day before yesterday that I was scoring my first goal in League football for Chelsea against the Tottenham team I used to support as a schoolkid? And wasn't it the day before yesterday that I scored in my debut for England in far-off Peru? And wasn't it just yesterday that I was appearing regularly on television with my Scottish sidekick Ian St John?

Blimey, doesn't tempus fugit when you're having fun. It's been the best seventy years of my life, so far ... and I hope I've got a few more miles to go yet.

When my mate Terry Baker told me he was going to write the truth about me I thought it was some sort of blackmail threat. But he genuinely believes that a book needs to be written that just sets out in black and white all the things I have been lucky (and occasionally unlucky) to have achieved.

The fact that he is being helped by Team Giller – Norman and his son, Michael – gives me confidence that it will be as accurate a book as can be written about me. Top writer Norman and I have been pals for more than 50 years, and I have known sports statistician Michael since he was a kid in short trousers. I remember having a kickabout with him in the garden at the Giller home some thirty or so years ago. I managed to kick the ball over the fence into the garden of a neighbour who usally refused to return the ball. Michael climbed up the fence and asked in time-honoured fashion: "Can we have our ball back, please." The miserable old git next door replied: "No, that will teach you to be more careful where you kick it."

Michael pleaded: "But it wasn't me, it was Jimmy Greaves."

The old boy said: "That sort of sarcasm just makes me more determined ..."

As he was chuntering on I put my head above the fence. He did not blink an eye and said: "Hello, Jim. Seen you play many times ..."

I have been fortunate in my choice of wife – the lovely Irene – and friends, and I am also lucky to have gathered a lot of fans along the way in my playing and after-football careers. Terry Baker, who I trust like a brother, will I know present the truth in this book without sensation or needless conjecture. That is why I have given the project my blessing, and I hope you enjoy the read.

More Than Just A Friend by *TERRY BAKER*

WHAT is it they say? 'Never meet your heroes. They can never live up to your expectations'. James Peter Greaves is my hero. I met him. I got to know him better than almost anybody else in his life. He exceeded all of my expectations and I am now proud to call him my close and dear friend.

My idol is now – quite unbelievably – 70-years-old, but aside from a comfortably spreading waistline and a couple of brand new knees you'd never know. In his company, you can still feel the presence of the sprightly young master skipping through defences and nonchalantly nestling the ball in the back of the net leaving a world-class 'keeper flat on his backside.

With the help of newspaper reports, statistics-that-never-lie and personal quotes from the man himself, I shall be sharing with you all the ups-and-downs, and the glory and the grief in the remarkable existence of England's most gifted forward.

I was also helped by the eye-witness reports of a mutual close pal of both Jimmy and myself, Norman Giller, who followed his career as a prominent Fleet Street reporter and has worked in harness with Jimmy on 18 previous books. My thanks in particular to Michael Giller, a chip off the old block who has followed his father as a sportswriting specialist, whose input to this book has been huge.

My first memory of Jimmy was as a seven year old. I settled down to watch my first Cup final on a huge TV cabinet with a tiny screen. Spurs v Burnley. Almost immediately he scored a great goal and became my favourite player. That was 48 years ago and my loyalty and opinion have never changed, He was/is the greatest goalscorer Britain has ever produced. It's indisputable because of the record books. At a time when defenders virtually assaulted great forwards, Jimmy took the kicks and elbows and carried on week in week out, year in year out, scoring some of the greatest goals ever seen.

Little did I dream in those far off days that I would get to work with my hero. I'd followed his trials and tribulations, never missed him on the telly and suddenly found myself booking him to do an after-dinner speech for my wife and business partner Freda and I in our home town of Bournemouth, where we mastermind our A1 Sporting Speakers agency, the best in the business (I would say that!).

I was so nervous I couldn't sleep. I shouldn't have worried; Jim and I hit it off almost

This is me, the middle man between my wife and partner Freda and my pal Jimmy

immediately and here we are fifteen years down the road as partners in a travelling road show during which Jimmy proves time and again that he has developed from awesome striker to one of the finest stand-up comedians in the land. We must have done 300 theatre shows together and he's still my hero in many ways.

Obviously I know him better than most in this stage of his life, and I can report that Jimmy remains funny, generous, tidy by nature, a natural performer, immensely talented at many things, loveable, loved, giving and now he's 70! His interests are vast; he is, for instance, a green-fingered gardener, a classy golfer and an expert on tropical fish. There is nobody quite like Our Jim.

There have been many books written by and about Jimmy. But this is the COMPLETE book, because nobody else has written about the great man as he reaches the allotted three score years and ten. I am telling the story in straightforward, unsensationalised chronological order because I want this to be a record of not only his career but of his life. Please join me now as I embark on a journey through the life-and-times of Jimmy Greaves – my hero and my pal…

King James surveys his kingdom in the summertime of his reign with Spurs

1: The Early Bird Catches the Goals

TUESDAY February 20th 1940 was the day the most natural goalscorer in the history of the Beautiful Game took his first kicks in the East Ham Hospital maternity ward. Just a few months after his first kick of life, Adolf Hitler and Hermann Goering started doing their evil best to flatten good old London Town, so Jimmy's Mum and Dad decided to move their new arrival away from the bombs and fire to the relatively safe haven of Dagenham.

With Irish blood and English heart, Jimmy was raised a Roman Catholic by father Jimmy senior and mother Mary. Home life was strict but blissful and Jimmy Snr., a Central Line driver on the London Underground, sowed the seeds for a love of football in his son from an early age.

An outstanding sportsman in his youth, Jimmy's Dad had played good-class football, hockey and tennis during Army service in India in the 1930s; and when he returned home he used to turn-out for three different football clubs a week.

Jimmy's father used to stud and dubbin junior's boots while Mum would wash and iron his kit. More importantly, his Dad spent hours making sure Jimmy could kick as accurately with his right foot as his natural left foot.

Within a few years, Jimmy was enjoying his first tastes of the fame that was to follow as a footballing prodigy on the streets of Dagenham and the playing fields of Southwood Lane Primary School and Lakeside Manor Boys Club.

Encouraged and cajoled by his inspirational schoolmaster Mr Bateman, Jimmy banged in scores of goals in the same easy manner later to be seen at stadiums all over the world. 'Ten-Goal-Greaves' would have been a fitting nickname for the young maestro and anything less than a hat-trick would be a sure sign that Jimmy was playing with a heavy bout of the 'flu.

Academically, Jimmy was not so prolific – a later diagnosis of chronic dyslexia being a major factor in his malaise – and an 11-Plus exam failure led to him attending Kingswood Secondary Modern School. His younger sister and brother, Marion and Paul, later became schoolteachers, a sure sign of the intelligence gene running through the Greaves family.

It was at Kingswood, a predominantly rugby-playing establishment that word began to spread of a special footballing talent. As a wicket-keeper/batsman, his cricketing skills also flourished – attracting the interests of Essex (makes you sick doesn't it?!).

Jimmy stepped up to the Dagenham Schools football first eleven and then Essex Boys. By the time he was selected for the London Schools side, the scouts had begun to gather like packs of wolves – not Wanderers!

During his time at senior school, and despite his reading troubles, Jimmy also began to excel with his class-work and had been made Head Boy. He was considered a viable candidate for further education, creating a welcome problem for his devoted parents about which path to take – football, cricket or higher learning. Thankfully, for us all, football won the day.

Jimmy senior and junior's favoured team, Tottenham Hotspur, were keenest to snap him up, but the sudden ill-health of legendary boss and Push-and-Run architect Arthur Rowe left the door open for Chelsea and West Ham to join the race.

His Dad always dreamed of Jimmy playing for the Lilywhites, but the persistence of Chelsea scout Jimmy Thompson (and a hush-hush fifty quid backhander in Irish notes) persuaded young Greaves to put pen-to-paper for the Blues of Stamford Bridge.

And so it came to pass that in April 1955, aged 15, Jimmy Greaves chose football, signed for Chelsea, the reigning League Champions, and the legend well and truly began…

Jimmy on his early life
'I have nothing but fond memories of my childhood. Mum and Dad always protected us from the harsh realities of financial worries and our house was full of love. Dad was my hero and best friend while Mum provided the much-needed discipline. Football was my life and I found it so natural to score goals. I had absolutely no idea how good I was – it was easy for me, to be honest. I now realise how lucky I was to be good at something I loved so much. Happy days!'

Frustration and disappointment marred the first couple of years of Jimmy's footballing life at Chelsea. The goals flowed in the youth team including a strike in his debut against Watford juniors. But senior team chances eluded our apprentice as he struggled to adapt to his early existence as a tiddler in the huge ocean that was life at a top First Dvision football club.

His junior coach, Dickie Ford, was well aware he was tutoring an extra special talent. But, as with all young footballers, there has to be a careful period of protection and development until all are sure they can cope with the pressures of life in the public spotlight. This led to a period of disillusionment for the raw, young prospect.

At one stage, Jimmy asked to be released from his contract and sought a normal life of work and part-time amateur football. Fortunately for our game in general and Chelsea in particular, this was a brief break and he was soon back at the Bridge biding his time, knuckling down and honing his already razor-sharp skills until he could be ignored no longer.

In the 1956-57 season, Jimmy netted an incredible 114 goals for the Chelsea youth team, including seven in one match. He was presented with an illuminated address marking the feat. His time had come.

Manager Ted Drake, the former Arsenal and England goal machine, selected Jimmy for a pre-season fixture in Holland which led to a League debut on the opening day of the 1957-58 season.

Fate decreed that his first match would be against Tottenham Hotspur, and so it was that on August 23rd 1957, 17-year-old Jimmy ran out on to the White Hart Lane pitch to embark on his First Division career.

After 86 minutes of a quiet, unremarkable debut and with Chelsea trailing 1-0, Jimmy burst into life and footballing legend. He received the ball 20 yards from goal and proceeded to dribble past John Ryden, Danny Blanchflower and Maurice Norman (not a bad trio to fox!) before calmly slotting the ball past goalkeeper Ron Reynolds. A point for Chelsea and a place in the following day's back-page headlines were Jimmy's rewards. Desmond Hackett, the eccentric master wordsmith in the brown bowler hat, wrote in the *Daily Express*:

> •Jimmy Greaves gave the greatest show I have ever seen from a young player in his League debut and I have seen the juvenile performances of soccer starlets Johnny Haynes and Duncan Edwards. Tottenham's Danny Blanchflower said after 17-year-old Greaves had snatched a late equaliser for Chelsea, 'The boy is a natural. He is the greatest youngster I have ever played against.'•

Five more goals in his next seven games were followed by a rare goal-drought in the Greaves career. Manager Ted Drake – building a team of young prodigies known as Drake's Ducklings – had been worried that Jimmy was getting too much publicity and pressure after he had gone a run of six games without a goal, and he was encouraged to take a complete break from the game.

It was supposed to have been a two-week rest but it stretched to more than a month

Jimmy on his way to the first of 357 First Division goals. It's his debut for Chelsea against Tottenham at White Hart Lane. That's centre-half Maurice Norman sitting helpless on his backside. By the time 17-year-old Jimmy had finished his demolition job, four Spurs defenders were on the floor. Spurs skipper Danny Blanchflower called it "a goal of sheer genius."

because Chelsea hit a winning sequence without Jim.

His recall to the first-team was the stuff of legend. These were the days when there was a full list of fixtures played on Christmas Day, and so it was that on December 25th 1957, Jimmy returned to the Chelsea team and helped himself to a festive feast of four goals in a 7-4 thrashing of Portsmouth at Stamford Bridge. Chelsea did not drop him again after that! The late Peter Lorenzo, then of the *Daily Herald,* wrote:

> •The phenomenal Jimmy Greaves gave Portsmouth a Christmas socking with four of Chelsea's seven goals at Stamford Bridge. It was a case of many happy returns for Greaves who had been rested by manager Ted Drake because "he's too good to hurry."•

By the way, trivia fans, this was Chelsea's last ever Christmas Day fixture.

The goals continued to flow and Jimmy finished his first season as Chelsea's top scorer with 22, including a hat-trick against Sheffield Wednesday.

That season, he also made his England Under-23 debut against Bulgaria at Stamford Bridge on September 25th 1957 and scored twice in a 6-2 England victory – can you see a pattern emerging here?

This seemingly unimportant match is worth mentioning in greater detail because it was the first time Jimmy played alongside his all-time favourite team-mate, Fulham pass-master Johnny Haynes. Jim Gaughan of that great old London evening paper, *The Star,* reported on the game:

> •More than 56,000 people at Stamford Bridge were shown that Johnny Haynes and Jimmy Greaves are natural partners. There has been nothing like this from an England pair since the great days of Raich Carter and Wilf Mannion. Greaves, making his Under-23 international debut, scored twice and missed a penalty during an eventful first match in which England crushed Bulgaria 6-2.•

Great praise and prophetic words indeed. Geoffrey Green, legendary football scribe at *The Times*, famously remarked that Haynes and Greaves 'was a partnership made in Heaven'.

In his personal life, 1958 was a year of pure joy for young Mr Greaves. In March of that year he married his childhood sweetheart, the lovely Irene Barden. The couple first met at a school youth club and were both just 18 when they wed at Romford Registry office in Essex. According to Jim and all close to him, the greatest achievement of his life was managing to capture the heart of the irresistible Irene.

Allow me a brief interlude now, especially for the attention of the younger readers, who may associate the life of a young footballing star with a world of WAGs, luxury cars, security-protected mansions and millionaire lifestyles. At that time – the era of the 'Soccer-Slave' and the maximum wage of £20-a-week – Jimmy was earning £17-a-week during the football season and £8-a-week in the summer!

The couple's first home was a one-room flat at Wimbledon's old football ground. Despite being Chelsea's top-scorer, money was still too tight to mention and the pair supplemented their income by weeding the Wimbledon terraces for £8-a-week, elevating Jimmy's off-season wage to a mighty £16-a-week.

Another indication of the status of the professional footballer that has changed beyond all recognition, is the fact that in 1958, Jimmy became one of the few players in the Chelsea squad to own a motor car. He bought his first vehicle, a 1937 Opel Convertible, for £30 from his brother-in-law. Life in the fast lane indeed!

 Jimmy on his Chelsea debut

'I remember before the game against Spurs having a pair of shorts thrown to me that came down past my knees. They would have been big enough for Bobby Smith, even Cyril Smith! But I was too nervous about the game to make any protest and from then on refused to part with those 'lucky' shorts. Everybody thought I was copying Alex James who had become a legend at Arsenal with his baggy shorts but it had not been planned.'

With Jimmy blissfully married and established as a rising star of The Beautiful Game, let us start our appreciation of Greavsie the goalmaster as, on the following pages, I give you a season-by-season, year-by-year account of the footballing phenomenon that was James Peter Greaves…

2: *Springtime for Chelsea and England*

The early summer of 1958 saw a concerted media campaign calling for Jimmy to be included in the England squad for the World Cup finals in Sweden. The tragic death of Manchester United's Tommy Taylor in the Munich disaster had left a huge hole up-front for the Three Lions. But the dinosaurs on the England selection committee considered Jimmy too young for such a high profile assignment and the up-for-grabs seat on the 'plane was filled by Wolves inside-forward Peter Broadbent, with West Bromwich Albion's Derek Kevan taking on Taylor's role as first-choice centre-forward. The selectors did have the foresight to take a young blond bomber called Bobby Charlton, and then failed to call him up to play a single game as England flopped out in the quarter-finals.

It would be another year before Jimmy's goals would make it impossible for the selectors to ignore him. In the meantime, he concentrated all his effort and focus into achieving another prolific season for The Blues. And what a start he made!

Just a couple of weeks into the new season, on August 30th 1958, Wolverhampton Wanderers were the Stamford Bridge visitors. Jimmy helped himself to five goals (with a good-looking sixth ruled offside) in a six-goal demolition of the reigning League champions. Such was the dizzying blitz inflicted on Billy Wright, that the 35-year-old England skipper decided that he would hang-up his boots for good at the end of the season. He later said: 'That was the day when I decided to give it just one more season. I realised I couldn't keep up with the pace of the First Division for much longer. Mind you, Jimmy gave every defender he came up against that season the run around. I always considered that his very best years were at Chelsea because he had no fear and just did what came naturally'.

There is a happy ending to this story for all supporters of the Wanderers as Billy's final campaign ended in Wolves glory with the Molineux club retaining their League title.

The wonderful Billy Wright would go on to play a big part in Jimmy's life and times. But more of that later.

Jimmy finished the season as the First Division's leading marksman with 32 goals, including a hat-trick against Nottingham Forest, the first brace of an incredible 24 League goals netted against the Reds of the City Ground during his career.

Unfortunately, as fast as Jimmy banged in the goals at one end, the Chelsea defence would open the doors at the back and let the opposition in. In the 1958-59 season, Chelsea scored 77 League goals and conceded 98 finishing 14th in the table. They were crazy days at The Bridge.

They used to have some ridiculous results in those days, giving ammunition to comedians who were always making Chelsea the butt of their jokes. After a 6-5 defeat, winger Frank Blunstone flung his boots across the dressing-room and complained bitterly to the defenders: "If we scored eight you could bet on you lot letting in nine." That anecdote comes from the mouth of Jimmy himself, who added: "Nobody disputed that Frank was right. It was like being at Butlin's, a real holiday camp atmosphere. Our lack of success did nothing to harm the dressing-room spirit, and even in defeat you would find us falling about laughing at things that went on at the club. We were still kids waiting to grow up."

In early May of 1959, Jimmy was finally given the recognition he deserved by the England selectors, earning a place on the summer tour of South America. Unfortunately, the trip ultimately resembled an escapade from a Carry On Abroad spin-off rather than a professional sporting tour. It was ridiculously organised and the travel schedule would have worn out even Marco Polo.

On May 17th 1959, Jimmy won his first England cap against Peru in Lima and – surprise, surprise – he scored with a neatly taken second-half goal. That was the only positive news in a match in which an ill-prepared and exhausted England side where comprehensively beaten 4-1.

David Jack, once a footballing master himself and writing for the long-gone *Empire News*, reported:

•Jimmy Greaves, making his international debut for England against Peru in Lima, scored the first of what will surely be many goals for his country. His performance was a rare bright spot in a humiliating 4-1 defeat that once again emphasised that drastic changes must be made at the top. Make no mistake, this is a crisis time for England. The game we gave to the world is no longer played with the required skill by English footballers.•

Nothing changes!

For the record, the England team that day was:

Hopkinson, Howe, Armfield, Clayton, Wright (Capt.), Flowers, Deeley, Greaves, Charlton R., Haynes, Holden

On that disastrous tour, England played Brazil, Peru, Mexico and the United States during a span of 15 days. They were beaten 2-0 by World Cup holders Brazil, 4-1 by

Peru, and then 2-1 by Mexico in the high altitude of Mexico City. They then regained a little pride with an 8-1 victory over the USA, with Bobby Charlton helping himself to a hat-trick. Three of the players in England's 18-man-squad – Roy Gratrix, Graham Shaw and Ron Baynham – travelled halfway round the world without kicking a ball and Wilf McGuinness played for only 45 minutes.

Jimmy's first experience of international football was a massive let-down but at least he returned home with his growing reputation intact. Now it was vital for our hero to get back to Chelsea, pick up where he left off and prove himself the master of goalhunters.

Jimmy on his early days at Chelsea

•What carefree days they were at Chelsea, both on and off the pitch! Ted Drake was a lovely bloke who will always be remembered for once scoring seven goals for Arsenal in a First Division match at Aston Villa. Ted had been bitten by the youth bug following the success of Manchester United's Busby Babes and used to send out a Chelsea team that was little older than a group of boy scouts. We were labelled 'Drake's Ducklings' and had more potential than any team I have ever played for. But you need experienced players to draw out the potential and we were just a bunch of kids playing it off the cuff and often coming off second best!

I must tell you a true story about Ted, who probably headed the ball too many times. He was once driving Terry Venables and me to the training ground, Terry sitting in front in the passenger seat. Ted droned on and on about tactical formations as we pulled up at a red light. He kept chuntering on and the lights changed without us moving. The bloke in the car behind quite rightly tooted us, and Terry said: "The lights have changed, Boss." Ted looked across at him and did a double take and then came out with the classic: "Bloody hell, I thought you were driving."•

3: *A Five-goal Feast at Preston*

THE 1959-60 Chelsea season began as the last had finished, with goals raining in at both ends, Jimmy scoring for fun, and the paying public – most of them standing on packed terraces – receiving amazing entertainment whenever Chelsea took to the field. After netting 11 goals in the early weeks of the campaign, including hat-tricks against Preston North End and Birmingham City, Jimmy scored just two in his next 11 matches. Press speculation was rife that the Greaves' goalscoring bubble had burst. I'll let Jimmy explain how he returned to form and silenced the critics in a mad day of mayhem in the return fixture against Preston at Deepdale on December 19th 1959:

‛It was one of those special days when everything I touched turned to goals. I scored an early hat-trick to put us 3-0 in the lead. I was a bit of a Jack the lad back then and, with the arrogance of youth, informed my team-mates, 'I've done my bit… now you lot have a go. I'm finished for the day.' By the time we were halfway into the second-half Preston had pulled back to 3-3 and skipper Peter Sillett said, 'Come on, Jim, you'll have to make a comeback.' I scored a fourth and then went into my shell again. Preston made it 4-4 and Peter pleaded, 'Just one more, Jim. That's sure to finish them off.' I duly scored a fifth to give us a 5-4 victory at Deepdale. That game sums up life at Chelsea in those crazy, crazy days.‛

Here's how James Connolly reported the match in the *Sunday Express*:

‛Jimmy Greaves, brilliant young Chelsea inside-left, toppled Preston off the top of the table with all five goals in a stunning success at Deepdale. Chelsea won a thrilling, see-sawing match 5-4, with all the glory belonging to Greaves who at times seemed to be playing them on his own.‛

The 1959-60 season was frustrating for Jimmy on the international stage. Once again, the selectors had no idea of their best team and Jimmy was in and out of the side. Joe

"Now listen to me Young Man ..." Yes, it's the one and only Brian Clough chatting to 19-year-old Jimmy during an England training session in 1959. They played in two internationals together, drew 1-1 with Wales and lost 3-2 to Sweden.

Baker, the Englishman from Hibernian with the broad Scottish accent, Manchester United's Dennis Viollett, Ray Parry of Bolton and one Brian Clough, vied with Greaves for roles up-front.

Jimmy scored against Wales in the Home International match at Ninian Park but saved his best international performance of the year for the England Under-23's against Scotland in Glasgow in March 1960. Bob Pennigton of the *Daily Express* penned: 'Magnificent, uncanny, superb, shattering. That was Jimmy Greaves at Ibrox last night with a hat-trick for Young England that was one of the finest seen in this hallowed home of Glasgow Rangers.'

Among Jimmy's team-mates that night were George Cohen, Maurice Setters, Peter Swan, Tony Kay, George Eastham and Bobby Charlton. Scotland included Adam Blacklaw, Jimmy Gabriel, Ian St John and Denis Law. What a cast!

Let us return to domestic issues. Once again, Jimmy finished a season as Chelsea's leading scorer with 29 goals. Dennis Viollett pipped him to the title of the Division's leading marksman with 32 League goals.

Chelsea finished the season in 18th position scoring 76 goals but conceding a whopping 91. Another season of profligate defending and unfulfilled potential was over and the feeling was that Jimmy was beginning to outgrow Chelsea – although his most prolific season in an amazing career was just around the corner…

Jimmy on growing up at Chelsea

❛I was getting frustrated by our inconsistency at Chelsea. It was good fun and I had a lot of laughs, but I was growing up and beginning to realise that I was not playing football for fun anymore. It was time for me to be more professional, but the way we leaked goals at Chelsea was becoming beyond a joke. Back in those days I had progressed from my 1937 Opel convertible to a 1938 Standard '8' and that became like a team bus, with all the players trying to crowd in after training sessions while we headed for the nearest pub for a pint. I drank no more, no less than other players then. To me a pint was the reward for a job well done.❜

In the opinion of most followers of The Beautiful Game – players, pundits and fans alike – 1960-61 saw Jimmy Greaves at the very peak of his extraordinary footballing powers. Off the pitch, it should have been an equally joyful time. He had a wonderfully happy and stable marriage, a beautiful young daughter, Lynn, and a second child on the way. By the end of the season, Jimmy's life was in turmoil.

Within four months of Irene giving birth to Jimmy Greaves Jnr, pneumonia took their beloved baby boy away. The tragedy ripped the heart and faith out of Jim and Irene and, to this day, their grief is still all too evident whenever they speak of 'Baby Jim.'

Talking to Jim now, he can trace this as the exact time when alcohol became a constant companion. He had always been a regular social drinker but now booze had become a means of escape from the realities of the present. This was the moment he took the first steps down the ladder to what would later become alcohol addiction.

At this time, Jimmy was also becoming disillusioned with the aggravating inconsistencies of football at Chelsea.

In the winter of 1960, Jim put in a transfer request. This is how the news was exclusively revealed by Clive Toye in the *Daily Express* in November 1960:

> •Jimmy Greaves, of Chelsea and England, the greatest goalscoring inside-forward of modern times, wants a transfer. He says: 'I want to try my luck with another club. Chelsea have great potential but, for some reason, it is not being properly fulfilled.'

Jimmy managed to pay off The Blues with a memorable last season of incredible goalscoring feats. He netted five goals against West Bromwich Albion at Stamford Bridge, four against Newcastle United at St James' Park and four in his farewell Chelsea game against Nottingham Forest at The Bridge (sorry again, Reds!). He also helped himself to hat-tricks against Wolverhampton Wanderers, Blackburn Rovers and Manchester City on his way to a stunning 41 First Division goals.

Goals just flowed from his boots in that final League campaign with Chelsea. Ralph Hadley, of *The People*, reported on December 4 1960:

> •Jimmy Greaves scored five goals in this 7-1 thrashing of West Bromwich Albion…the 12th time he has scored three or more in a match. He has become the youngest player at 20 to total 100 League goals and has scored 11 times in 11 appearances for England. How on earth can Chelsea even think of selling him? It would be like selling off the family silver.'

Tom Holley, also of *The People*, reported on another Jimmy goal spree at St James' Park on March 25 1961:

'A wonder show of goal snatching by Jimmy Greaves just about put paid to Newcastle's hopes of staving off relegation. He crashed into top gear with four brilliant goals as Chelsea helped themselves to six in twenty-eight fantastic minutes. I have seen all the top British goal scorers of the last three decades and there have been none in his class as a player who can turn a half chance into a goal in the twinkling of an eye.'

Jimmy's final season at Chelsea saw a peak of the end-to-end chaos at The Bridge. The Blues finished a respectable 12th scoring 98 goals. Unfortunately, their Keystone Cops approach led to them conceding 100!

The story of Jimmy's unrest and eventual move to Milan could fill three books – one a story of espionage and skulduggery, another a classic farce, and the third a tale of darkly comedic irony. Let me try to clarify the situation as briefly as possible:

Shortly before his four-goal haul at St James' Park a Newcastle official privately told Jim the club would pay him a signing-on bonus of £1,000 and give him a £50-a-week car salesman job if he agreed to join them. Tapping-up a new phenomenon in football? I don't think so!

Around the same time, Joe Mears, the late Chelsea chairman and one of football's great gentlemen and administrators, telephoned Jimmy to say there was a chance of him moving to Italy because an embargo on foreign players was about to be lifted there at the end of the 1960-61 season. Mr Mears wanted to know if he was interested. With no maximum wage in the 'Land of the Lire' Jimmy's response was 'When does the plane leave?'

Soon afterwards, Jimmy was contacted by an Italian journalist acting as an 'undercover agent' for an unnamed Italian club offering him a private deal, thus bypassing Chelsea's official channels. After a clandestine meeting in a Soho restaurant, the club was revealed to be the giants of AC Milan.

Being a man of honour, Jimmy advised the journalist to tell Milan to make a direct approach to Chelsea. He may have been a slave in those days but he was loyal to his masters.

Chelsea and Milan held hush-hush talks and before Jimmy knew it, he was whisked

A rare picture from Jimmy's scrapbook ... captain Greaves! He was about to make his final appearance for Chelsea against Nottingham Forest at the Bridge and is seen shaking hands with Forest skipper Bobby McKinlay, against whom he then went and scored four goals!

off to a private Italian hospital in the heart of London for a thorough medical check-up. After being passed 100% fit everything was set for Jim to sign.

Giuseppi Viani, AC Milan's manager, and the negotiating agent Gigi Peronace travelled to London to clinch the deal. Jimmy was offered a £10,000 three-year contract, with a £1,000 down payment the moment he signed – a small fortune for any footballer in those days. Chelsea's consolation for selling Jim would be £80,000. Not a bad profit on a player who had cost them just a £10 signing-on fee (plus the hush-hush £50 in Irish fivers). Jimmy duly signed and was committed to join AC Milan at the end of the season. It was then a record fee received by an English club, although Torino were soon to top that figure when buying Denis Law from Manchester City for £100,000.

While they were negotiating their money-making moves to Italy, talks were progressing between the Jimmy Hill-propelled PFA and the Football League in an effort to abolish the days of Soccer Slavery and the £20 maximum wage. With strike action threatened, the PFA won the day and a new era of money-making for the men who mattered dawned in the English game.

Jimmy had signed his soul away to Milan for self-confessed mercenary reasons. Money was the only motive and he soon realised that, aged just 20, he was now completely out of his depth. His immaturity showed in the way he reacted to receiving the £1,000 signing-on fee from Milan. He immediately went out and blew it on a year-old Jaguar. To this day, he's still a sucker for a fast, flash motor is our Jim! Quite a step-up though from the 1930s Standard 8.

With Jimmy's ink still wet on the Milan contract, Cockney comedian and Fulham chairman Tommy Trinder boldly announced: 'Johnny Haynes is a top entertainer and will be paid as one. I will pay him £100-a-week to play for Fulham.' According to Jim, this was the funniest line Tommy Trinder ever delivered and his good pal Johnny Haynes was laughing all the way to the bank.

Over the next few months, Jimmy and a team of friends, colleagues and advisors including Jimmy Hill, Joe Mears, England boss Walter Winterbottom and FIFA President-to-be Sir Stanley Rous tried everything possible to find a way out of the Milan move. It was all to no avail. The Italian giants tightened their grip with an improved contract and there was no way out. And so it was to be, with a cruel twist of irony, just as the money started pouring into the English game, Jim was moving out.

On April 29th 1961, Jimmy played his final match in a Chelsea shirt, the goal feast against his rabbit team Nottingham Forest at Stamford Bridge. After scoring all four goals in an exciting 4-3 victory, captain for the day Jimmy was carried shoulder-high around the pitch by fans. There was hardly a dry eye in the house.

A happy and joyous finale at Chelsea? Not quite. The club then decided they wanted him 'one more time' in a meaningless end-of-season friendly in Israel. Jim refused to make the trip and Chelsea slapped a 14-day ban on him that deprived him of an England cap in an international against Mexico at Wembley. Mention this to Jimmy today and the annoyance is still palpable.

On the international stage, 1960-61 was a breathtaking year for Jimmy. In eight matches he hit the back of the net 13 times. It's no coincidence that these were the first games played in tandem with his future White Hart Lane strike partner, the rugged-yet-skilful Bobby Smith. As Bobby was fond of saying: 'I knock 'em down and Jimmy knocks 'em in!'

The highlight of that (and any other) season was undoubtedly the 9-3 massacre of the 'Old Enemy' Scotland at Wembley on April 15th 1961. Any members of the Tartan Army are advised to skip the following section of our story (Dave Mackay will definitely refuse to read it). Frank Butler reported in the *News of the World:*

> •There are some who will say Jimmy Greaves is worth £200,000 after the way he strolled through this 9-3 humiliation of Scotland at Wembley. He scored three goals and played a major role in three more.•

Let me hand over to Jim for his thoughts on the demolition of the Scots just two weeks before Mackay helped Spurs become the first team of the century to complete the League and Championship Double

Jimmy on the slaughter of the Scots

•The real star of that pulsating performance against a Scotland side including Dave Mackay, Denis Law and Ian St John was our skipper Johnny Haynes, who paralysed the Scots with his pin-point passes. He got two goals himself, as did Bobby Smith. Bryan Douglas and Bobby Robson scored one each. An abiding memory is of Dave Mackay charging murderously at any Englishman in possession in the closing stages of the match. He carries the scar of that demoralising defeat to this day. England came close to perfection that afternoon. The pity was that we failed to reach double figures. That would have been a magic entry in the record books.•

The crushing win was a vindication of a team policy that team manager Walter Winterbottom had adopted at the start of the season. He was determined to mould a settled side and pledged to keep the team unchanged provided, of course, everybody was fit and playing reasonably well. He kept to his word and England scored 45 goals in nine international matches!

At the end of the slaughter of the Scots, England players carried Johnny Haynes around the pitch on their shoulders as if he was the FA Cup. For the record, the England line-up on that memorable day:

Springett, Armfield, McNeil, Robson, Swan, Flowers, Douglas, Greaves, Smith, Haynes (Capt.), Charlton R.

And so we reach the end of a tumultuous season of personal and professional extremes for Jimmy. With bags and emotional baggage packed, Jimmy is about to reluctantly embark on his adventure to foreign fields…

Jimmy on the Italian Job

❝Italy! At the time it was like someone saying, 'Would you like a share in a gold mine?' I was earning the maximum £20-a-week while in Italy football players were picking up small fortunes. My Italian vocabulary didn't reach much farther than 'spaghetti bolognese' but I was ready to shout 'Si! Si! Si!' all the way to the bank! I was a married man with a daughter and another baby on the way. Twenty pounds a week was not going to pay for the bright future I had mapped out for my wife and family. Irene and I had already been through hell together. Just a few weeks earlier we had lost our beautiful four-month-old son, Jimmy. It was a nightmare experience that nearly drove Irene and me out of our minds. A move to Italy sounded just the change of scenery and surroundings we needed. Oh well, as they say – you live and learn.❞

4: Misery in Milan on the Way to Tottenham

THE Milan adventure began well enough. Jimmy flew out in June 1961 to make his debut in a prestige friendly against Brazilian giants Botafogo. With Irene expecting again, it was agreed that he could then return to London for the birth, due the following month.

Once again, Jimmy scored a debut goal in a 2-2 draw. The fans took to him straight away and the officials said they looked forward to his return in July after the baby had arrived. All on the surface was friendly, but then relationships quickly soured.

With their child reluctant to make an entrance (eventually the gorgeous Mitzi), Jimmy delayed his scheduled journey back to Italy. It could have been called a pregnant pause. He cabled Milan to tell them he would be staying with his wife until the baby was born. They showed a great sense of understanding by threatening to fine him £50 for every day he failed to make an appearance. From that moment on, there was no way Jimmy Greaves and AC Milan were going to get along.

With Mitzi finally born on August 6th, Jimmy was able to fly out for his new life in Italy. He was in for a mummy and a daddy of a telling off.

Between his signing for Milan and joining them, they had taken on a new coach, the strictest of strict disciplinarians Nereo Rocco. Within days, the two were at war. Rocco decided the best way to handle his new forward was to be as tough and cruel as possible. Jimmy's answer was to rebel and make life hell for his coach.

The pre-season training camp in the remote outpost of Galaratte was run like a prison camp. The training drills were regimented and repetitive, food and drink were rationed – drinking beer was considered a mortal sin - and socialising outside the camp was strictly forbidden unless accompanied by Rocco.

The harsher the discipline, the harder Jimmy battled for his freedom.

During his four months in Italy, Jimmy scored a more than respectable nine goals in 14 matches, often playing as a lone striker. But he hated every second of the football. The Italian game was dominated by stifling Catenaccio (translated as door-bolt) tactics and Jimmy was a regular victim of shirt-pulling, spitting, off-the-ball brutality and suffocating man-to-man marking.

Off the pitch, things went from bad to worse. Rocco and the AC Milan officials decided the best way to pull Jimmy into line was to fine him. An unauthorised

It's the Milan derby 1961, and Jimmy is reunited with his England team-mate Gerry Hitchens, star striker with Inter Milan. They used to meet in secret for quiet drinks together, otherwise Jimmy would have been fined for 'consorting with the enemy.'

sightseeing trip to Venice with Irene cost Jimmy £500 and a death-defying visit to the team hotel bar via an outside balcony with his brother-in-law Tom Barden incurred a £300 penalty.

On one occasion, Jimmy and Tom were spotted relaxing and drinking lager on a hotel balcony. The following day, two workmen went to his room and nailed planks of wood across the door leading to the balcony.

Something had to give and, eventually, Rocco accepted defeat and Jimmy was let loose. The Jimmy Greaves Club was formed – its members a group of journalists and friends who spent many memorable nights helping Jimmy to drink Milan dry. They had club ties made, patterned with the initials JG, a map of Italy and, perhaps fittingly, a load of balls.

With some of his team-mates now refusing to pass to him during matches, vicious attacks by the Italian press and not-so-secret plans to replace him afoot, Jim's days in Italy were numbered.

Chelsea and Tottenham Hotspur were two of the clubs eager to bring our homesick hero back to Blighty. Considering a return to Stamford Bridge a backward step and wanting to compete for some silverware, Jim accepted a £60-a-week offer from the Lilywhites of White Hart Lane. Milan tried to play Chelsea and Spurs off against each other to get the fee up, but Bridge chairman Joe Mears (through his mouthpiece, club secretary John Battersby) and Bill Nicholson came to a private agreement not to get involved in an auction. Once Jimmy had made it clear he wanted to sign for Spurs, 'Gentleman Joe' graciously stepped to one side. It was certainly not a decision driven by money, because Chelsea had been prepared to pay him £120 a week, astronomical money at a time when the average national weekly wage was £10 a week.

 **Jimmy on coming home**

⁶I was coming home not for financial reasons, but peace of mind and wanting to play for a club I had always wanted to play for going back to when I was a schoolkid. The Milan adventure was not something I would have wished on my worst enemy. If it had not been for Rocco, perhaps I would have found it a more enjoyable experience. But he and I just collided and it soured everything. All I wanted to do was get home.⁹

On November 18th 1961, Jimmy officially became a Spurs player. Legendary boss Bill Nicholson did not want him saddled with the label of the League's first £100,000 footballer and so did a deal at the memorable price of £99,999.

Five days later, shrouded in a thick blanket of fog, Jim climbed into his Jaguar and headed for the airport. The nightmare was over and the golden summer of Jimmy's career was about to begin…

On his return to England, cash-strapped Jimmy and his family temporarily moved in with his in-laws. Whoever thought he had come back from Milan a millionaire was about a million pounds out in their assumption.

Before he could make his League debut at White Hart Lane, Jimmy had to undergo a League inquiry into possible irregularities in his transfer. Welcome home Jim! After being totally exonerated of any wrongdoing, he was free to resume his career.

When Jim joined Spurs the players were initially wary of him. They had been reading the day-by-day accounts of his exploits in Italy and must have been thinking that he was nothing but a troublemaker. Having just won the League and Cup double without him, it would have been understandable if they looked on him as an intruder who could possibly rock their happy and successful boat.

It took just a couple of training sessions and two goals in a reserve team game at Plymouth Argyle (watched by a crowd of 13,000) to kick their doubts into touch. He settled into the Tottenham way of doing things – both on and off the pitch – as if he had been at White Hart Lane all his life.

On December 16th 1961, Jimmy ran out at The Lane in front of 45,000 fans to make his much-anticipated debut for Spurs. What followed has passed into footballing folklore. Blackpool were the unfortunate opponents as Jimmy helped himself to a stunning hat-trick in a 5-2 Spurs victory.

Jim considers his first goal in the 39th minute as one of the greatest of his illustrious career.

This is how Victor Railton of the London *Evening News* described the game:

> •Jimmy Greaves made a sensational start to his career with Spurs this afternoon with a hat-trick against Blackpool at a packed White Hart Lane. So he kept up his habit of always scoring on a big occasion debut. One of his goals was of the classic variety only he can produce. It came from an overhead scissors kick after Terry Medwin had flicked on a long throw from Dave Mackay. The Spurs supporters loved it and gave Greaves a great ovation.•

From that moment on, Jimmy was accepted by the Tottenham players and fans alike as 'one of them'.

Playing for a disciplined, crack outfit was a revelation for Jimmy. Every single player in the squad was exceptional. Cliff Jones, John 'the Ghost of White Hart Lane' White and Bobby Smith were truly world-class. Add to them the all-time legends that

Jimmy strikes with a rare headed goal at The Lane, watched closely by John White.

were Dave Mackay and Danny Blanchflower and you have a sublime, purring Rolls Royce of a team.

In 1961-62, Spurs came oh-so-close to eclipsing their historic achievements of the previous year. They finished third in the First Division, just four points behind surprise champions Ipswich Town, and were robbed of a place in the European Cup final with a perfectly good-looking Greaves goal waved offside in the second-leg of a classic semi-final encounter against Benfica at The Lane.

Here's how Roy Peskett reported the injustice in the *Daily Mail* on April 5th 1962:

> ❝Jimmy Greaves, whose 'goal' in the 23rd minute was disallowed for offside, protested after Benfica had beaten Tottenham 4-3 on aggregate in the European Cup semi-final. The angry young man told me: "I ran between two Benfica players before shooting, so how could I possibly have been off side? It was definitely a genuine goal."❞

The FA Cup was now the only chance for Jimmy to win his first major trophy in professional football. Spurs reached the final with a string of vibrant, exciting performances.

In the first round, Jimmy scored twice in a 3-3 draw against Birmingham City at St Andrews. A 4-2 victory in the replay with another Greaves goal took Spurs into the second round. From then on it was smooth sailing. They sank Plymouth 5-1 and then West Bromwich Albion 4-2 with Jimmy netting twice in each game.

Alan Hoby of the *Sunday Express*, reported:

> ❝Incredible Tottenham Hotspur yesterday reached the last eight in the FA Cup when they beat West Brom before 55,000 stunned and astonished spectators. We saw two jinking Greaves goals, both of them great and both of them so memorable that they will be relished and cherished like old brandy.❞

A comfortable 2-0 quarter-final victory against Aston Villa at The Lane set up a dream semi-final against Man United at Hillsborough that Spurs won 3-1 at a canter, with Jim contributing a little gem of a goal.

Tony Pawson, once a maestro with Pegasus, reported in *The Observer*:

> ❝Spurs went marching serenely on to the FA Cup final at Wembley, untroubled by Manchester United or the strains of the European Cup. Jimmy Greaves took his vital goal with a sleepwalker's casual certainty, waiting for United goalkeeper Gaskelll to dive, then sliding the ball gently under him.❞

On May 5th 1962, Spurs and Burnley lined-up on the hallowed Wembley turf to contest the FA Cup final. Spurs got off to a dream start against an exceptional Burnley side that had pipped them to the runners-up place in the League title race by one point.

The game was barely three minutes old when goalkeeper Bill Brown belted a clearance upfield to Bobby Smith, who nodded it to Jimmy. Travelling at full pace, Jim briefly overran the ball. Nimbly skidding to a halt as he regained control had the effect of throwing the five back-pedalling Burnley defenders ahead of him off balance. Jimmy spotted an unguarded path to goal and steered the ball all the way along the ground past each of them and into the corner of the net just wide of the fingers of goalkeeper Adam Blacklaw. The finish was as precise as a Tiger Woods putt and, when you watch the footage today, it perfectly portrays the genius of Jim.

After Jim Robson equalised for Burnley early in the second-half, a cracker from Bobby Smith and a Danny Blanchflower penalty clinched victory for the mighty Spurs.

Jim had won his first major winners' medal and the joy on his face as he joined his team-mates on a lap of honour holding the famous old trophy showed how much it meant to our hero. In total, Jimmy had scored nine goals in seven FA Cup ties in 1962. He had certainly earned his medal. The Spurs line-up:

Brown, Baker, Henry, Blanchflower, (capt.), Norman, Mackay, Medwin, White, Smith, Greaves, Jones

Jimmy on his instant Wembley goal
●Watching the old (very old!) footage of my FA Cup final goal against Burnley, I can't believe how slowly the ball seemed to roll into the net. I was never a blaster of the ball. I always envied the way players of my era, such as Bobby Charlton and Peter Lorimer could hammer shots in from 30 yards – these days I suppose you'd mention players like Rooney, Gerrard and Cristiano Ronaldo for their power. I couldn't burst a paper bag from a range of more than 15 yards. But accuracy and precision were my specialties. That goal was one of the most satisfying of my career and it gave me particular pleasure because before the game I had made a pledge to my team-mates that I would score a goal within five minutes. It was not like me to make such a rash promise, but I just wanted to give myself extra motivation for what was one of the most important matches of my career.●

Artist Art Turner captures Jimmy on a Wembley lap of honour with Bill Brown, Danny Blanchflower, Dave Mackay, John White and Cliff Jones

The victory over Burnley earned Tottenham a place in the European Cup-Winners' Cup but, before that famous campaign, there was the small matter of the 1962 World Cup finals. Hardly pausing for breath at the end of an exhausting season, Jimmy set off for Chile with the England squad.

They stopped off on the way for a warm-up game in Peru, as Desmond Hackett reported in the *Daily Express* on May 20th 1962:

> Jimmy Greaves, at his glorious best, scored a first-half hat-trick here against Peru to set England off to a goal-studded start as they head for the serious business of World Cup campaigning in Chile. On this form, 'Jinking Jimmy' could be the hidden ace that trumps the more fancied sides in the finals.

Unfortunately, the World Cup proved to be a competition too far for several of the England players after an overworked season at home left many of the squad, including Jim, weary and homesick before a ball was kicked in the finals.

The England preparations were embarrassingly unprofessional. They travelled without a team doctor, and at one stage manager-coach Walter Winterbottom was reduced to having to go into the kitchen of their spartan, remote training camp because the food being served by the Chilean chef was too spicy for English tastes.

The squad was stuck away in a mining village halfway up a mountain, and boredom was a worrying factor that the blazered brigade at the Football Assocation had not considered when planning the build-up to the World Cup. Professional players were being treated like schoolkids, and Jimmy found he was suddenly thrust back in the suffocating atmosphere that had been such a turn-off in Italy. Like so many exceptionally talented footballers, Jimmy was a free spirit and he had the prisoner feeling again that had made his life a misery in Milan.

England were uninspired and lack lustre and lost 2-1 to Hungary in their opening match, before producing an impressive performance to beat Argentina 3-1 – including Jimmy's one and only goal in a World Cup finals tournament. A dull and turgid 0-0 draw against Bulgaria led to a quarter-final showdown with the holders, the legends of Brazil, at Vina del Mar on June 10th 1962. Two strikes from the great Garrincha and one from Vava, with an England consolation from Gerry Hitchens, resulted in a 3-1 victory for Brazil – a scoreline that quite frankly flattered the tired and outclassed Three Lions.

There was a bizarre incident during the game that will always link the names of Jimmy Greaves and Garrincha. A stray dog invaded the pitch during the first-half, and it led a posse of players and ball boys a merry dance before Jimmy got down on all fours to capture it. The intruder seemed very relieved when carried to the touchline.

Too relieved in fact. He rewarded Jim by sending a yellow stream running down his England shirt and shorts.

Garrincha, an animal-loving country boy, fell in love with the stray and evidently saw the pooch as a lucky omen, because he took command of the match after it had trespassed on the pitch. He adopted the dog, named it Jimmy Greaves and took it home to Brazil with him!

Brazil – even without the injured Pele – went on to retain the World Cup with a 3-1 victory over Czechoslovakia in the final, while Jim and his fatigued colleagues travelled home to recharge their batteries in readiness for the challenges of the new season.

Jimmy on the 1962 World Cup

•When you think what I had been through the previous ten months or so it was little wonder that I did not have the right appetite or attitude for the 1962 World Cup finals. What I needed was rest rather than having to play against the greatest teams in the world. They stuck us away out of sight and sound of civilisation, and managed to get us bored out of our minds before the opening match against Hungary. We played well against Argentina, but even had we been at the top of our form we could not have lived with that great Brazilian team in which Garrincha was stunning. Pele always gets the vote as Brazil's King, but Garrincha was not far behind him. He was completely unpredictable, and played like Stanley Matthews on speed. He was a complete freak, who wore two left boots. His speed was phenomenal and if he was in the right mood – he was a moody git – he could take the tighest defence apart with dribbling and ball control that was magical to watch, provided you were not on the receiving end. If he was playing today the bidding for him would start at around seventy million quid. Yes, he was that sensational.•

5: *Conquering Europe with Super Spurs*

TOTTENHAM's pulsating performance in the annual Charity Shield curtain-raiser on August 1st 1962 was an appetiser for what was to come in the months ahead. League champions Ipswich Town were put to the sword at Portman Road by a rampant Spurs side, refreshed and high on confidence following their FA Cup triumph in May. The final score was 5-1 with strikes from Terry Medwin, John White and Bobby Smith plus two from Greaves the goal machine. Spurs were off and running and ready for action.

Jimmy was at his fluent best with nine goals in the first ten games of the League campaign when his favourite whipping boys, Nottingham Forest, visited White Hart Lane on September 29th 1962. A crowd of 49,075 gathered at The Lane to witness another astonishing performance by Greaves and the Lilywhites. Jimmy rattled in four goals as they romped to a 9-2 win.

Bill Holden of the *Daily Mirror* reported:

'Jimmy Greaves led Tottenham on an incredible nine-goal spree against Nottingham Forest, demonstrating his wide variety of scoring methods. He headed the first goal, calmly side-footed his second and fourth – and raced through to hit a tremendous drive on the run for his third.'

Four weeks later, Jimmy and Bill Nicholson's wonder-team were at it again, this time demolishing Manchester United 6-2 at White Hart Lane.

Clive Toye reported in the *Daily Express*:

'Super Spurs looked Britain's answer to Santos, Brazil's World Club champions, as they slapped Manchester United to the bottom of the First Division last night. Leading the goal glut, of course, was Jimmy Greaves. He scored three and hit a post as Tottenham romped to a 6-2 triumph.'

In November 1963, Jimmy netted twice against Gordon Banks, the Leicester City goalkeeper he bracketed with Pat Jennings as the best he played with or against. One of the goals brought him a standing ovation which echoed in the press box.

Alan Hoby, of the *Sunday Express*, reported:

> *Jimmy Greaves scored one of the greatest goals I have ever seen before 52,000 applauding spectators in the sunshine and joy of White Hart Lane yesterday. He did a swaying, dribbling ballet dance past four stupefied defenders. Then, drawing goalkeeper Gordon Banks out of goal with another effortless swerve, Greaves calmly placed the ball into the empty net. Everyone of us rose to applaud this wonderful solo effort.*

A Boxing Day hat-trick and a goal-double in the two League fixtures against Ipswich, two goals against Blackpool, and strikes against Burnley, Birmingham, Leicester, Leyton Orient and Fulham kept Jimmy at the top of the goalscoring charts and Spurs in contention for the League championship.

As the title race entered its finishing stretch, one last League game of that sublime season deserves eulogising. On April 15th 1963, 53,727 spectators packed into The Lane to watch Spurs take on Liverpool.

Bill Shankly was still some way off completing the construction of his first great Liverpool side, but a team containing Ron Yeats, Ian Callaghan, Roger Hunt and Ian St John would surely provide formidable opposition? Not a chance! On this particular afternoon, the Reds were humbled 7-2 with Jim cashing-in with four goals.

Brian James reported in the *Daily Mail* :

> *Like a king travelling incognito, with glimpses of majesty again and again shining through, Spurs moved a shade farther ahead of the common herd in the chase for the championship crown yesterday with this 7-2 victory against Liverpool. Master marksman Jimmy Greaves provided a four-goal flourish as Tottenham topped a hundred League goals for the season.*

With the League campaign running smoothly, the quest to become the first British club to win a European trophy was proving to be spectacular – with a succession of memorable evenings crackling with electric atmosphere at White Hart Lane. To this day, anyone fortunate enough to have attended those spine-tingling nights, will tell you they were the most exciting ever experienced at a British ground.

Given a bye in round one, Spurs were drawn against Glasgow Rangers in a mouth-watering 'Battle of Britain' second-round tie. In the first-leg at White Hart Lane, Jimmy took on the roles of provider – creating three goals from pin-point corners in a comfortable 5-2 Tottenham victory.

In the return match in Glasgow, a baying crowd of 80,000 witnessed two Bobby Smith goals and a wonder strike from Jim that contributed to a 3-2 Spurs win and an overwhelming 8-4 aggregate triumph. The match had been billed as the 'Club Championship of Great Britain,' and nobody was left in any doubt that Tottenham were the superior side.

Ken Jones, cousin of Tottenham wing wizard Cliff Jones and himself a former professional, reported in the *Daily Mirror:*

⁹Jimmy Greaves, Spurs' ace goal-snatcher, tore the heart out of every fan who boasted the bold blue of Rangers with one moment of majesty at Ibrox Park. Greaves swept out of a tackle and then thrust through from the halfway line to hammer home the goal that virtually killed this European Cup-Winners' Cup tie. Make no mistake about it, that ruthlessly executed goal was the killer. Greaves is the sort of exceptional player who does not just decorate games, he also decides them. He naturally scores the sort of goals others can only dream about. Every time he touched the ball the Rangers defenders were exposed to the perils of panic.⁹

The one and only blip on Tottenham's march to the final came in the first leg of the quarter-final clash with Slovan Bratislava. Spurs went down to a worrying 2-0 defeat, but managed to turn it around at the Lane, with Jimmy scoring twice in a comprehensive 6-0 victory.

One of Jimmy's favourite tales is of how Bobby Smith gave Tottenham a psychological advantage at the end of the first leg in Bratislava. He made an 'I'll have you at home' gesture to the centre-half who had been giving him a bit of a rough time. Then he put a clenched first under the goalkeeper's nose and said with a heavy Northern accent: "Londres ... Londres ... you'll get yours in Londres."

It may have lost something in its interpretation but the message was not lost on the goalkeeper, who literally turned white. He knew what was coming. And Smithy did not disappoint him. He charged the goalkeeper into the back of the net in the opening minute, this in the days when you could shoulder charge goalies without risking being put in the Tower. The poor bloke lost all his appetite for the game, and Spurs slammed in six goals.

The semi-final first-leg against OFK Belgrade in the capital of the old Yugoslavia, saw Jimmy again making headlines – this time for all the wrong reasons. In a feisty, often brutal affair, he was sent-off for the one and only time in his professional career.

Jimmy on his early bath

'OFK had been ultra-defensive and nasty with it. There were boots flying and they were giving us plenty of stick. So Dave Mackay and Bobby Smith started to even things out a bit. I cannot think of two blokes I would rather have on my side in a rough-house. It was due to Smithy's enthusiasm – for the want of a better word – that I got sent for an early bath for the first time in my career. Going for a ball, his elbow caught their centre-half in the stomach. It really took the wind out of the bloke and he went down on his knees. I stood looking on quite innocently when suddenly this feller jumps up and comes at me like a bull. He wasn't a bad judge picking on little me, rather than the massive Smithy. Anyway, he threw a punch and missed and I immediately threw one back – and missed. I was never any good at counter-punching. The Hungarian referee saw the whole incident but chose to pick on me. And with 45,000 Yugoslavs screaming blue murder, who could blame him! I could hardly believe it when he gave me my marching orders. What hurt most of all was that I had not even had the satisfaction of making contact with my attempted punch. The crowd were going mad, throwing bottles and abuse. Cliffie Jones, who had been sitting on the sub's bench, escorted me off the pitch with a protective arm around my shoulders. 'Come on Jimbo,' he said, his eyes shining with excitement. 'I'll see you're all right. Let 'em all come at us. We can take 'em.' Cliffie's Welsh blood was boiling and he was enjoying every second of it. Me, I was frightened stiff!'

Spurs had the last laugh, beating OFK 2-1 and then, minus the suspended Jimmy, completing a 5-2 aggregate victory with a 3-1 win at The Lane.

On May 15th 1963, Tottenham Hotspur took on Atletico Madrid in the European Cup-Winners' Cup final at the Stadion Feijenoord in Rotterdam. History was beckoning. If they could beat the holders Atletico they would become the first British team ever to win a major European tophy.

Spurs were dealt a hammer blow shortly before the kick-off when the inspirational Dave Mackay failed a fitness test. The news for everybody in the Tottenham camp could be measured on the Richter scale. Mackay was the heart of the team, indominatable and feared by defences across Europe.

The normally unflappable Bill Nicholson was so depressed by Mackay missing the match that in the pre-match team talk he was full of pessimissim. He built up Atletico Madrid as the greatest team he had ever seen. The impression he gave the Spurs players was that the Atletico defenders were as big as mountains and would crush any forward silly enough to go near them, and he made their attack sound as if they had five forwards with the skill of di Stefano and the shooting power of Puskas. Bill was trying to guard against any risk of complacency, but he had overplayed it and – according to Jim – managed to frighten the players to death.

It was left to skipper Danny Blanchflower to deliver a speech of Churchillian tones to rally the troops – and what a job he did! He picked up the Tottenham players by telling them how good they were and that the Atletico team would be dreading facing them. Danny's motivational team-talk worked wonders. Mackay's understudy Tony Marchi was outstanding, Terry Dyson had his greatest game in a Spurs shirt and, of course, Jimmy's finishing was clinical and classical. It was an epic night as Spurs dominated Atletico and captured the Cup with an emphatic 5-1 victory.

Ken Jones reported in the *Daily Mirror*:

Spurs won the European Cup-Winners' Cup here in Rotterdam tonight with this five-goal massacre of Atletico Madrid and so became the first British club to carry off one of Europe's top soccer trophies. This was a night of personal glory for impish wingman Terry Dyson and goal ace Jimmy Greaves who both netted twice.

The Spurs side on that historic, all-conquering night:

Brown, Baker, Henry, Blanchflower (capt.), Norman, Marchi, Jones, White, Smith, Greaves, Dyson

A Glory Glory night in Rotterdam as skipper Danny Blanchflower is paraded around the pitch after the European Cup Winners' Cup victory over Atletico Madrid. Left to right, Cliff Jones, Tony Marchi, Bobby Smith, Peter Baker and goal-scoring heroes Terry Dyson and, on the extreme outside, Greavsie.

Jimmy on Terry Dyson's delight

•No question about who was the man of the match – Terry Dyson, who played out of his skin. He scored two cracking goals and was always running the Atletico defence into a blind panic. As he came off at the end Bobby Smith grabbed hold of him and said, "If I were you Terry I would announce that you are retiring right now. You will never be able to top that. It was one of the proudest nights of my footballing life. I had joined Tottenham because I wanted to win silverware, and here we had the first major European trophy ever picked up by a British team. They can't take that moment of history away from us. And to think we managed it without our best player, Dave Mackay.•

Spurs went into the final games of the League campaign neck-and-neck with Everton in the race for the championship. But fighting on two fronts proved too much for the Lilywhites, and a draw and two defeats in their last three matches meant that the League trophy was Goodison-bound.

Jim gained some personal consolation by once-again topping the First Division scoring table with a remarkable 37 goals to add to the five precious goals he scored in Europe.

On the England circuit, Walter Winterbottom bowed out as boss in November 1962. The team gave him a fitting send off in his last match in charge with a 4-0 victory over Wales at Wembley – Jimmy scoring the final goal of the Winterbottom reign. In Walter's place came a former Tottenham hero from the Push and Run era, Alf Ramsey, who had grown up in the same Dagenham area as Jimmy. He had proved himself an exceptional club manager by guiding a team of Ipswich veterans and misfits to the League championship. Now he had been charged with the job of trying to bring the World Cup to the home of football when staged in England in 1966.

Ramsey's reign began in ignominious fashion with a 5-2 humiliation against France (when goalkeeper Ron Springett kept losing the ball in the glare of the poor floodlights) and a 2-1 defeat to Scotland at Wembley, when Slim Jim Baxter completely bossed the game for the Old Enemy.

Much has been written about Jimmy's relationship with Sir Alf but I can honestly say, with hand on heart, that I have never heard Jimmy utter a negative word about the great Knight of the Beautiful Game. They were both from the same Essex territory but as alike as grass and granite. Alf was a quiet, serious-minded man who was not exactly what you would describe as good humoured, and he was obsessed with football tactics, hence his nickname The General in his Spurs days; Jim, of course, was rarely interested in talking in-depth football tactics and did things off the cuff and was always bubbling company. Let it be a matter of record that they liked each other, despite what you might hear from the gossips.

Jimmy finished the 1962-63 campaign rightfully regarded as a true goalscoring phenomenon of the game and good enough, at the age of just 23, to be favourably compared to all-time England legends such as Bill 'Dixie' Dean, Tommy Lawton, Nat Lofthouse, Jackie Milburn and Stan Mortensen.

While Jimmy was at the top of his game, Tottenham would never again quite reach the peaks of those golden years…

 **Jimmy on his halcyon days at The Lane**

⁶If a man's life is as the four seasons, then there is no question that I had my summertime at Tottenham. I am ready to argue with anybody that this Tottenham team was one of the – if not the – best club team in post-war British football. I get goose pimples just thinking about some of the football we used to play. It was out of this world. We enjoyed ourselves on and off the pitch, and in those days I had my drinking under control. It was fun!

We worked hard on the pitch and played hard off it. Don't interpret that as meaning we were a load of playboys. We enjoyed a drink and a laugh at the bar. That was playing hard in those days when nightclubs were few and far between. There was a great team spirit and it really was all for one and one for all. When you had leaders on the pitch like the brainbox Blanchflower and the warrior Mackay you did your best to match their standards. At our peak, we were among the Great Untouchables. Now we had a European trophy to prove that we were unbeatable on a bigger stage, but it still wrankles that we did not pick up the European Cup the previous season. We were cheated out of it by poor decisions. That's my story, and I am sticking to it.⁹

THE 1963-64 season dawned with no hint that it was to see the break-up of the Super Spurs in tragic circumstances. All good things come to an end, but the way the team that Bill Nicholson built disintegrated was both cruel and heartbreaking for everybody involved with the club – players, backroom team and supporters.

Jimmy started the season in prolific form, helping himself to yet another hat-trick against Nottingham Forest on August 31st. Pat Collins – father of virtuoso sports columnist, Patrick – reported in *The People*:

> **The biggest difference between Tottenham and Forest was Jimmy Greaves. Only he, with his uncanny goal flair, could so dramatically change Tottenham's pedestrian performance into a solid 4-1 win. And only he could have scored such a cheeky hat-trick.**

In the following months of the campaign, Jim scored 13 goals in 17 League games including three-goal hauls against Blackpool and Birmingham City.

All was rosy on and off the pitch for Jim. On October 31st. Irene gave birth to their third child, Danny, named after his Godfather Danny Blanchflower. A real chip off the old block, Danny went on to become a prolific marksman with the Tottenham youth team, Southend and then Cambridge before injury brought his promising career to a premature halt.

At Old Trafford on December 10th, Spurs suffered their first serious setback of the season. In the second-leg of a European Cup-Winners' Cup tie against Manchester United, Dave Mackay was seriously injured in a collision with Noel Cantwell that must have left the United captain wondering about the validity of his challenge. Mackay was carried off with a broken leg and the heart of the Tottenham team went with him.

It would be 18 months before Mackay would return to the first-team after beaking the leg again in his comeback match, and while he would remain a formidable presence on the field, the era of Mackay the 'Buccaneering Braveheart' was sadly over.

Soon after, Danny Blanchflower was forced to retire because of a recurring knee injury. Now Super Spurs had lost both the brains and the heart of the team.

Through all the upheaval, Jim still managed to bang in the goals at will and Tottenham sat proudly at the top of the First Division early in the New Year.

On January 11th 1964, Spurs overwhelmed Blackburn 4-1 at White Hart Lane with Jim once again in fine form. Joe Hulme, pre-war Arsenal legend (and briefly Spurs manager) reported in *The People*:

> 'The lethal finishing of Jimmy Greaves put Spurs on top of the First Division. Greaves was the match-winner against Blackburn with a hat-trick that was Jimmy at his immaculate best. I played with and against the best finishers of the 1930s, and Jim can be compared with any of them, including the likes of Dixie Dean and Hughie Gallacher.'

Eventually and inevitably, the absence of Blanchflower and Mackay took its toll and Spurs ran out of steam, finishing the season in fourth place – six points behind champions Liverpool. With 35 goals, Jimmy topped the First Division scoring charts for the fourth time in his career.

On the international front, Alf Ramsey had quickly settled into his role as England mastermind and was making early progress on his way to finding his first-choice eleven for the home World Cup finals in 1966. Gordon Banks was firmly established as the No 1 goalkeeper and, with Jimmy Armfield injured, George Cohen had grabbed the right-back role, with Ray Wilson immovable on the left-side of defence. Completing the back-four at that time, were captain majestic Bobby Moore and Tottenham rock Maurice Norman. Further forward, the only two certainties on the team-sheet were Bobby Charlton and one James Peter Greaves.

A busy and challenging year for the Three Lions saw them play 11 internationals – winning seven, drawing one and losing three. The two highlights of the winter campaign were a prestige fixture against a star-studded Rest of the World side to commemorate the Centenary of the Football Association and a home international against Northern Ireland – the first match played under floodlights at Wembley.

The Rest of the World squad that lined-up at Wembley on October 23rd 1963 read like a who's who of footballing legends of the era, including Yashin, Kopa, Law, Di Stefano, Eusebio, Gento, Baxter, Seeler, Puskas. In such illustrious company, the star of the show in a 2-1 England victory was, inevitably, Jimmy.

Lev Yashin dives at the feet of Jimmy during the Rest of the World match in 1963

Distinguished footballer writer Brian James reported in the *Daily Mail*:

'A century of English soccer has ended. It drew to a fitting close at Wembley with a final 90 minutes that saw skill and courage create an England victory against the Rest of the World to be taken and held proudly high. This, above all, was Jimmy Greaves's greatest match. The quick wit and quicker aim of the deft, little Londoner have never before been spurred by such zeal for combat. It was his goal four minutes from time that put the seal of triumph on this historic match that marked the FA Centenary. He might easily have had a first-half hat-trick but for some out of this world saves by Russia's spiderman of a goalkeeper, Lev Yashin.'

The only challenger to Jim for the Man of the Match plaudits was Denis Law, who played for the Rest of the World team with flair and fire and was rewarded with their equalising goal before Jimmy popped up with the winner.

Jimmy on the Russian Grand Master Yashin

'There are those who will tell you that Lev Yashin was even greater than our goalkeeping masters Pat Jennings, Gordon Banks and Peter Shilton. He made three blinding saves against me, but I managed to get the ball past him once after a 20-yard run through the defence. Scottish referee Bobby Davidson disallowed it because he had blown for a free-kick in my favour after I had been fouled just outside the penalty area. He apologised for not playing the advantage rule. I described it as the greatest goal I never got! It was great to see my mate Denis Law having an outstanding game for the Rest of the World, and he outshone the stars surrounding him. When I at last got the winner Yashin had been replaced by Yugoslav goalie Soskic. So I did not have the satisfaction of beating the Russian wonder man.'

The following month, England demolished Northern Ireland under the newly installed Wembley lights. Jimmy helped himself to four goals and Southampton winger Terry Paine scored a hat-trick in an 8-3 England win.

Ken Jones was there for the *Daily Mirror*:

'England, a ruthless, goal-hungry England, rubbed the face of Irish football into the green turf of Wembley. Four goals by Jimmy Greaves and a Terry Paine hat-trick are the jewels that will sparkle in the memory. Veterans in the Wembley Press Box were unanimously of the opinion that they have not seen a more clinical finisher than Greaves.'

An end-of-season 'Little World Cup' tournament in Brazil brought England crashing back down-to-earth with a thud. Jimmy scored a consolation goal as they were humbled 5-1 by a Pele-inspired Brazil. A subsequent 1-1 draw with Portugal followed by a 1-0 defeat to Argentina meant that it was back to the drawing board for Alf and his team.

Back at home, Tottenham suffered the cruellest and most heartbreaking tragedy of their Annus horibilus. On July 21st 1964, John White was sitting under a tree sheltering from a storm on a North London golf course when he was fatally struck by lightning. Spurs had lost a great player and Jim had lost a good friend.

Within the space of seven short months, Bill Nicholson and his team were suddenly forced into facing a future missing the three most vital cogs of the Tottenham machine.

The combination of an ageing squad, appalling injuries and one terrible tragedy had ripped the heart-and-soul out of the team and led to a period of rebuilding at The Lane.

Jimmy on the the Golden Trio

'It was the three-man midfield engine-room of that team in the early Sixties that set us apart from every other side. Danny Blanchflower was the poet of the team. He gave us style and panache and was a captain in every sense of the word. The late, lamented John White was so aptly named the Ghost of White Hart Lane. It was his ability off the ball that made him such a phenomenal player. He would pop up from out of nowhere just when he was needed to make a pass or collect the ball. Like Danny, he had the gift of being able to give the exact weight to a pass so that the ball would arrive where and when you wanted it. Completing the trio was Dave Mackay. If somebody held a gun to my head and insisted that I name the greatest player in that outstanding team, it would have to be the swashbuckling Dave. He had just about everything: power, skill, drive, stamina and, above all, infectious enthusiasm. With Blanchflower, White and Mackay together in midfield we just could not go wrong. I strongly believe the combination of those three great, great players has yet to be matched in the English game. To lose them all in one season, particularly the tragic death of John, was almost too much to bear.'

There were a host of new faces at White Hart Lane as the first kicks of the 1964-65 season were taken. Having already added Alan Mullery from Fulham and Laurie Brown from Arsenal to his squad, Bill Nicholson was once again busy in the transfer market.

Cyril Knowles from Middlesbrough, Pat Jennings from Watford and Jimmy Robertson from St Mirren were the latest additions. In December, Alan Gilzean joined Spurs from Dundee. An audacious bid to bring pass master Johnny Haynes to North London from Fulham ultimately failed.

In the following year, Mike England – from Blackburn – and Terry Venables – Chelsea – were signed to complete the rebuilding at Spurs.

The 1964-65 campaign began with Jimmy scoring in the first two games of the season, but the Tottenham form was patchy as the new-look side understandably struggled to gel.

Occasionally, they clicked and everything fell into place. The home fixture against Burnley was such a game. Desmond Hackett got carried away with his report of the comprehensive Spurs victory in the *Daily Express* on September 2nd 1964:

> ❛The author of Tottenham's 4-1 win against Burnley was Jim 'The Genius' Greaves. I have seldom seen him play with such skill, such industry and such admirable effect. This was world-class soccer at its peak, and it was the crafty Cockney with the Artful Doger goal-picking talent who looked as good as any of the Brazilians, the Hungarians or, come to think of it, the Martians. What an England captain Greaves would make in this wondrous, world-beating mood. He would lead with style and a smile.❜ – Steady on, Des!

On September 19th, Jimmy scored his 100th League goal for Spurs against West Bromwich Albion. Joe Hulme reported in *The People*:

> ❛Jimmy Greaves was back at his magnificent goal-grabbing best to spark Tottenham's fifth successive home victory. He scored the only goal of the game – his hundredth League goal for Spurs – and might have finished with five but for a super display by West Brom goalkeeper Ray Potter.❜

The arrival of the elegant Alan Gilzean from Dundee just before Christmas was a defining time in Jimmy's career at Spurs. At last, he had found a strike partner to fill the mighty boots of Bobby Smith. Gilly was not a physical player like Smith, but all guile and style with a unique gift for glancing headers. He had amazing close ball control, and explained that he had perfected it in his days as a schoolboy in Scotland. "We used to have one ball and thirty kids playing in the street," he said. "If you were lucky to get your feet on the ball you had to be sharp and skilful to keep it."

Greaves and Gilly – the 'G-Men of Tottenham' – went together like bacon and eggs and formed an association that was always prolific and truly fantastic to watch, such was their understanding of each other's game. They were also quite a formidable pairing in the pub!

Alan Gilzean, through the eyes of graphics illustrator Art Turner

As the season entered its final weeks, Greaves and Gilzean were at their best when Blackburn Rovers were squashed 5-2 at White Hart Lane on April 16th 1965. The report I found in Jimmy's scrapbook on that match was written by Norman Giller in his days as chief football reporter for the *Daily Express*:

> ⁶Three goals from Alan Gilzean and two from Jimmy Greaves against Blackburn tell their story of another slaughter by the mighty G-men of Tottenham. This was Gilzean's first three-goal haul for Spurs – but it could not rob Greaves of the man-of-the-match rating. Jimmy ran the Rovers defenders into dizzy disarray, and might easily have doubled his goals tally.⁹

Spurs ended the 1964-65 season in sixth place with Jimmy, inevitably, finishing as the First Division's top scorer with 29 goals. There were no League hat-tricks for Jimmy. He saved his three-goal performances for the FA Cup – against Torquay United in a third-round replay at Plainmoor and in the following round against Ipswich at The Lane. Malcolm Gunn reported the 5-0 dismantling of Ipswich in the *News of the World*:

> ⁶Ipswich were demolished by the £170,000 firm of messrs. Greaves and Glizean, goal contractors extraordinary. Greaves scored three and Gilzean two in what was a White Hart Lane walk-over.⁹

A combined value of £170,000 for Greaves and Gilzean? What would they be worth today? The mind boggles! Together, they would have to be worth in excess of £70-million

Tottenham's promising FA Cup run ended in the fifth round with a 1-0 defeat to Chelsea at Jimmy's old hunting ground of Stamford Bridge.

England remained unbeaten throughout the 1964-65 international season with a series of solid if unspectacular performances resulting in six victories and four draws.

The one remarkable match of the campaign was the first of the season which saw the Three Lions take on Northern Ireland at Windsor Park on October 3rd 1964. Playing only his third match in Irish green was a young, snake-hipped prospect by the name of George Best.

Jim scored a stunning first-half hat-trick in 11 minutes as England rushed to a 4-0 half-time lead, but the second-half belonged to Best and Ireland. The young Manchester

United winger tied the England defenders in knots, and inspired the Irish into a fight back that had England hanging on for a 4-3 victory at the final whistle.

Jimmy's hat-trick took his England tally to 35 and led to another entry in the record books, as he became England's all-time leading goalscorer.

By the end of the year, three more pieces of the Ramsey and England World Cup jigsaw had fallen into place. Jack Charlton had replaced Maurice Norman as first-choice centre-half and 'Toothless Tiger' Nobby Stiles had made the midfield ball-winner role his own. Not the most positive strides forward for the football purists among us! – But there's no doubting that Jack and Nobby added some much-needed steel and spite required by any country aiming to make a successful bid for World Cup glory.

The other new face was that of baby-faced Blackpool midfield dynamo Alan Ball, who proved a revelation in an England shirt with his all-energy performances.

Two prospective England World Cup squad members had ruled themselves out of contention by being dragged into a scandalous, headline-hitting match-fixing scandal. Tony Kay and Peter Swan were among 10 current and former players found guilty and jailed in a dark episode for the game.

With Jimmy and England in fine form and fettle, all was set for the final build-up to the 1966 World Cup. Surely nothing could possibly stop Jim from being a major player in the England quest for the Jules Rimet trophy.

Meantime, Bill Nicholson was trying desperately to piece together a Tottenham team in the same mould as the great Double side. He was like a man who had once been in love with the most beautiful woman in the land, and was now trying to find a look-alike. But his current model was not quite as eye-catching as the earlier one.

How different might it have been had be landed Johnny Haynes from Fulham following the tragic death of John White? By rights the England pass master should have joined Tottenham from school. He was a local lad playing for Edmonton schoolboys, but somehow he missed the Spurs net and signed for the Craven Cottage club because his best pal Tosh Chamberlain was there and said how friendly it all was.

Bill Nicholson thirsted to pair Haynes with Jimmy Greaves after he saw how they brought the best out of each other, first for England Under-23s and then the full England team. Fulham chairman Tommy Trinder had stifled Italian interest in Haynes by making him the first £100-a-week footballer in English football, and when Bill Nicholson came knocking with a big cheque in his hand Fulham resisted. They reluctantly allowed Alan Mullery to make the switch to White Hart Lane but Johnny Haynes was not for sale at any price.

Jimmy on the remodelled Tottenham

❛I was disappointed that Bill Nicholson failed in his bid to bring Johnny Haynes to Tottenham as John White's successor. Haynesie and I had an almost telepathic understanding at England level. We could read each other like a book and always knew exactly where to position ourselves on the pitch to get the best out of each other. Bill Nick was trying to build another 'Super Spurs'. He never quite made it. The new Tottenham team had some great moments together but we never touched the peak performances of the Blanchflower–White–Mackay era. Alan Mullery and Terry Venables took over in midfield but I never felt really content and comfortable playing with either of them. Both were given a tough time by the Spurs supporters, who had been spoiled over the years and unkindly kept comparing them with their great idols, Blanchflower and Mackay. Mullers and Venners were both keen students of the game, and although neither of them actually said anything to me, I sensed they would have liked me to have been more conventional and conformist in my approach to football. I liked them both, respect them as outstanding players and thought they talked a lot of sense about the game but I've always closed my ears to too much tactical theory.❜

7: *A Jaundiced View of the World Cup*

THE 1965-66 campaign began with Jimmy at his absolute best. The two main men in his professional life, Bill Nicholson and Alf Ramsey, must have been enjoying stress-free nights of deep sleep, safe in the knowledge that the goal-getting responsibilities were unquestionably taken care of in that momentous year.

The stand-out performance in those early months of the season was fortunately captured for posterity by the *Match of the Day* cameras. The mighty Manchester United were the visitors to White Hart Lane on October 16th 1965, as Spurs and, in particular, Jimmy hit top form.

He made two and scored probably his most famous goal as Tottenham dismantled the 'Red Devils'. Veteran reporter Maurice Smith reported in *The People:*

'The ringleader of Tottenham's 5-1 victory against Manchester United was Jimmy Greaves – back in the act as Lord Jim. Flooding out a tide of defence-splitting passes, he made the way for the first two goals and snatched the third after beating four men inside the space of his own hall carpet.'

Please treat yourselves and take five-minutes to watch the goal highlights on YouTube. The black-and-white footage does nothing to diminish the quality of a breathtaking goal that perfectly portrays what Jim was all about. Reporters did not check their watches for this goal. They checked the calendar, because it will be remembered for years to come. Nobby Stiles, Pat Crerand and Bill Foulkes were among the quality defenders that Jimmy took to the cleaners on the way to a goal that featured in the *Match of the Day* opening credits until the introduction of colour five years later.

All was progressing smoothly on the pitch as Jim netted 11 goals in the first 14 matches of the season. On the home front, the Greaves clan was completed with the birth of his fourth child, the bonny baby boy Andy.

With his personal and professional life in splendid order, little did Jim realise that the first cruel twist of fate that was to turn his great year into a nightmare was just around the corner.

With the gift of hindsight, you can pinpoint Guy Fawkes Night, 1965 as the fateful evening when Jimmy's World Cup hopes and dreams began to go up in flames – excuse the pun.

When lighting a bonfire in the garden for his kids, Jimmy felt the early symptoms of what he thought was the 'flu and took himself off to bed. Within days, he was diagnosed with hepatitis B – a dreadful, debilitating liver infection that saps the energy and strength from its victims for months.

While lying jaundiced in hospital, Jim received the distressing news that Tottenham centre-half Maurice Norman had broken his leg in a meaningless friendly against a Hungarian Select XI at White Hart Lane. It was a double-fracture of tibia and fibula, and would end Big Mo's distinguished career during which he won 23 England caps as a commanding defender who played a key role in the glory glory days of 'Super Spurs'. He would have been a shoe-in for the England No 5 shirt in the 1966 World Cup. His bad news meant a big step forward for Jack Charlton, who had been living in the shadows of Maurice and Peter Swan, who had got himself jailed and banned following the bribes scandal.

It would be three months before Jimmy would return to the Spurs first-team and, at least a year – the most important year – before he completely shook off the after-effects of the illness.

Jimmy on his illness and rehabilitation:

⁶I can still remember that awful feeling on bonfire night when I realised I was really ill. It was if somebody had chopped me off at the legs. I have never worked harder in my life to recapture fitness, even cutting right back on my drinking. This was a time of my life when I could control myself. I was desperately keen to play in the finals because I was convinced England were going to win. Everything was right for us. We had a great pool of players, vital home advantage and the right mood running through the game at League level. People who considered that I was not interested in playing for my country obviously did not know that I had a burning ambition to help England win the World Cup. That hepatitis attack robbed me of a vital half-yard of pace but I still believed I was good enough and sharp enough to represent England better than any other striker around. That may sound conceited but any goalscorer who lacks confidence and belief in his own ability is in trouble. I believed in myself and I know that Alf Ramsey thought I was the right man for the job.⁹

On January 29th 1966, Jimmy made his First Division comeback at White Hart Lane and scored from the penalty spot in a 4-0 Spurs victory over Blackburn Rovers. He went on to score a further four goals, two of them from the spot, as stuttering Spurs ended the season in a disappointing eighth place.

All concentration was now focused on the World Cup as England completed their build-up to the finals. Because of his illness, Jim missed five internationals, during which time Roger Hunt and Geoff Hurst had both found the net – ousting Joe Baker and Alan Peacock from the England set-up.

Greaves returned to the international stage on May 4th, in England's last match at Wembley before the finals. They beat Yugoslavia 4-0 with Jimmy looking back to his best. He scored after nine minutes and produced an impressive. eye-catching performance. His place in the squad was secured. The match was notable for featuring the outstanding debut of Martin Peters, the player who would be described by Alf Ramsey as 'ten years ahead of his time'. Everything was falling into place.

Four wins followed in four final warm-up games in Europe, including a 6-1 thrashing of Norway with Jimmy finding the back of the net four times. His place in the World Cup starting XI was sealed and England were ready.

The quest for the World Cup began, as so often happens, with a sterile, defensive 0-0 draw in the opening match between England and Uruguay. With nine Uruguayan men behind the ball at all times, there was no space to be found by Jimmy and the afternoon ended in frustration for all Englishmen.

In their second match, goals from Bobby Charlton and Roger Hunt and an assured showing from Jim resulted in a 2-0 victory over Mexico.

A draw in their final group game against France would secure the hosts a place in the quarter-finals. With England leading 1-0, courtesy of a Roger Hunt goal, Nobby Stiles launched – let's call it – 'an enthusiastic challenge' on French playmaker Jacques Simon. The enraged Simon sought revenge but thought better of taking on our Nobby. His closest alternative target was innocent bystander Greaves who received a raking studs-first kick. The assault left Jimmy nursing a badly gashed left shin.

Unaware of the seriousness of his injury, Jimmy played on little-knowing that his World Cup was running on borrowed time. A further Hunt goal handed England a comfortable 2-0 victory and ensured their progress to the knockout stages. While the rest of the team celebrated, Jim was in the treatment-room receiving four stitches to his gashed shin.

With Jimmy unfit for the quarter-final clash with Argentina, Geoff Hurst was called-up into the first-team.

The rest, as they say, is history.

Just for the record – and for anybody purchasing this book as a gift for an alien relative on their home planet – Geoff scored the only goal of the quarter-final with a classic made-in-West Ham headed goal against Argentina, the perfect cross provided by Martin Peters. Jimmy watched from the stands with the rest of the non-playing squad as the match deteriorated into farce, with Argentine captain Antonio Rattin getting sent off for disputing just about every decision that the German referee Rudolf Kreitlein made. Even the usually composed Alf Ramsey lost his rag, and became a hate figure

It's the morning after the third World Cup match against France, and Jimmy is describing his injury to reserve goalkeeper Ron Springett at the England headquarters in Hendon, with Bobby Moore looking – as ever – immaculate.

throughout South America for describing the Argentinians as animals.

Jimmy's shin injury was not responding to treatment, and Alf decided to select an unchanged team for the semi-final against Portugal, for whom Eusebio had been in sensational form. He scored four goals after North Korea had taken a 3-0 lead over Portugal in the quarter-final at Goodison. But they were not a one-man team. Jose Torres was a towering inferno at centre-forward and skipper Mario Coluna was a dynamic force in midfield, and they had the thrust and skill of Augusto and Simoes.

England produced their best performance of the finals, beating Portugal in a classic contest thanks to two beautifully taken goals by Bobby Charlton, who was at his brilliant best as a deep lying centre-forward. Euesbio scored Portugal's goal from the penalty spot, the only goal that England had conceded on the way to the final. The match was a personal triumph for Nobby Stiles, who (perhaps literally) marked Eusebio out of the game, a feat he was to repeat two years later in the European Cup final.

The newspapers were now full of conjecture as to whether Jimmy would play. His stitches were out and he was fit enough to train on the Thursday before the Saturday final. Everybody had an opinion as to whether England's greatest modern goal scorer should be selected. Only one man knew the answer, and Alf Ramsey was saying nothing.

Quietly the night before the final Alf told – in confidence – each of the players he had decided would play that they were in. He wanted them to go to sleep worrying about playing rather than worrying whether they would be picked. Not a word was said to Jimmy, who was room sharing with his best pal Bobby Moore.

On the morning of the match Jimmy packed his bags ready to make a quick getaway as soon as the Final was over. He was going on a family holiday with Irene, and brother-in-law Tom Barden and his wife, regardless of whether he played.

He still did not know whether he was in. Around mid-day Alf called a team meeting and read out the side for the final: Banks, Cohen, Wilson, Stiles, Jack Charlton, Moore, Ball, Hunt, Bobby Charlton, Hurst, Peters. An unchanged team, the side that had carried England through the quarter and semi-finals.

Jimmy, along with the other ten players left out, shook hands with those selected. There was a strong team spirit, and the good luck wishes were genuine. Just for the record, these were the players who did not make it along with Jim: Springett, Bonetti, Armfield, Byrne, Flowers, Hunter, Eastham, Connelly, Paine, Callaghan.

That afternoon Geoff Hurst – July 30 1966 – scored the most famous hat-trick in history, with Jimmy looking on from high in the stands. He did not even see Geoff's hat-trick-completing ("They think it's all over ...") goal because, along with the rest of the non-playing squad, he was making his way down from high in the Wembley stand to take part in the after-match celebrations.

Bobby Moore shook hands with the Queen and lifted the Jules Rimet Trophy after an epic 4-2 win over West Germany. It had been the greatest week – culminating in the greatest day – in English football history. And it had all happened without the greatest forward of the modern game. Sorry Jim ... not that he has every sought sympathy, and has shown his character by shurugging it off 'as one of those things ... good luck to Geoff.' It is a nonsense to say that it drove him to drink. He was already drinking more than his fair share long before the World Cup.

Jimmy on missing out on World Cup glory

❝Alf quite properly preferred a 100% fit player for the quarter-final against Argentina and Geoff grabbed his chance magnificently. At the end of the Portugal semi-final I felt in my bones that Alf was not going to select me for the final. I was fit for selection and the Press boys began churning out, 'Greaves must play' or 'Greaves must not play' stories. But only one bloke knew for sure whether I was going to make it – Alf Ramsey. And he wasn't saying a dickie bird.

The Saturday of the final came and I still did not know for sure whether I was in or out. I was a *Daily Express* reader and noticed that my mate Norman Giller said Alf should pick an unchanged team. Thanks Norm. I sensed that Alf was being a little distant and guessed he had made up his mind to go with a winner side. I knew for certain at mid-day and I had guessed right.

People have often asked me since what Alf had to say to me when he told me I was out of the side. What could he say? He knew I was choked but he was doing what he believed to be right. There were 10 other blokes in the squad as unlucky as me, so there was no reason why Alf had to sort me out for a special word of sympathy. Not that I was seeking anybody's sympathy. I felt sorry for myself and sick that I was out. But I was not and never have been in any way bitter against Alf. He did his job and England won the World Cup.

After the final, I danced around the pitch with everybody else but even in that great moment of triumph I felt a sickness in my stomach that I had not taken part in the match of a lifetime. It was my saddest day in football.

As the celebrations got into full swing I quietly returned to the hotel, picked up my bags and slipped off home. Bobby Moore later told me that Alf thought I had deliberately snubbed him after the game but that is far from the truth. I was delighted for Alf and didn't want to spoil his moment of glory by letting him see the hurt in my eyes.

I went home and quietly got drunk. Late that night I went off on a family holiday. The 1966 World Cup was suddenly history.❞

8: Mackay lifts the FA Cup at Wembley

THE 1966-67 season began just 21 days after England's World Cup triumph. Everybody in the country was still riding the huge wave of euphoria and a large dose of that good feeling was spreading round White Hart Lane as Spurs, and a fully recovered Jimmy, made a smashing start to the new term.

An opening day victory against Don Revie's formidable Leeds United – with Jimmy on target in a 3-1 triumph – was followed by seven wins in their next ten outings. It was in that opening match against Leeds that Dave Mackay made his comeback after twice breaking his leg, and the famous photograph was taken by *Daily Mirror* photographer Monte Fresco of Dave giving Leeds bruiser Billy Bremner a chilling warning that he had better watch his tackling.

The highlight of Tottenham's outstanding start, was a 3-1 home triumph over deadly rivals Arsenal that handed early-season North London bragging rights to The Lane faithful. Victor Railton reported in the *Evening News* of September 3rd 1966:

> ❛Arsenal's unbeaten run ended at White Hart Lane this afternoon when they went down to slick Spurs. Cliff Jones gave Tottenham a first-half lead and Jimmy Greaves neatly found the net in the 57th and 69th minutes to prove he remains the best goal poacher in the business.❜

As summer gave way to autumn, the Lilywhites sat proudly on top of the First Division, with Jimmy helping himself to nine goals in the first 11 games of the season.

A run of five losses and a draw was to follow, dashing their dreams of another League triumph. It was an increasingly familiar inconsistency in form that has continued to frustrate Spurs fans to this day – prove me wrong, Harry.

In typically contrary fashion, Tottenham could now concentrate on the FA Cup.

They began their FA Cup campaign with a tough third-round tie against the hard men of Millwall at The Den. As always, Spurs received a hostile reception both on the pitch and from the terraces and rode their luck to escape with a 0-0 draw. As the cliché goes, every team needs a little luck in a long Cup run and Spurs had used up a fair share of theirs in this tough fixture.

In the replay at The Lane, the lithe, light-footed Alan Gilzean scored the only goal

Artist Art Turner's view of the Dave Mackay warning to Billy Bremner. Jim, who was looking on, said: "Bremner turned as white as a Lilywhite shirt. I think Dave got his point across!"

of another tight, tense affair. Spurs had scraped through to the next round.

The fourth round saw Tottenham drawn at home to Portsmouth and the G-Men were at it again. A crowd of 57,910 watched Alan Gilzean score twice and Jimmy net the third as Spurs progressed to the last 16 with a comfortable 3-1 win.

Jimmy was on target again in round five with Bristol City the unfortunate victims at White Hart Lane on March 11th. Greaves scored both goals – one from the penalty spot, in a 2-0 victory as Tottenham swept into the quarter-finals.

A sixth round pairing with Birmingham at St Andrews in round six looked a tricky prospect for Spurs, and they were more than happy to shut-out City and take them back to The Lane after another goalless draw. In the replay on April 12th, Tottenham hit top form and piled six unanswered goals past the outclassed Blues. Jim and Terry Venables helped themselves to two goals each, with Alan Gilzean and Frank Saul completing the scoring. The great old trophy was now within touching distance.

Only semi-final opponents, Nottingham Forest BC – Before Clough – could now stop Spurs from reaching an FA Cup final for the fifth time in their illustrious history. On April 29th the two teams walked out at Hillsborough in front of 55,000 spectators and proceeded to serve-up an end-to-end thriller of a semi-final.

Cyril Knowles was the early Tottenham hero, clearing a Frank Wignall header off the line – nice one, Cyril. Chances were created at both ends, with Gilly and Greaves going close for Spurs while a smashing leap and header by John Barnwell saw the ball just clear the Tottenham bar.

Spurs took control of the game with two brilliant strikes either side of the half-time interval. In the 32nd minute, a first-time pass from Knowles fell perfectly to Jimmy as he found himself in space 20-yards from goal. With his lethal-left foot, Jimmy struck a first-time shot on the half-volley and the ball screamed past the despairing dive of Forest 'keeper Peter Grummitt and into the net off the left-hand post. It was a rare long-shot goal from Jimmy's golden boot.

After 66 minutes, Frank Saul made it 2-0 to Spurs with an unstoppable drive from the edge of the box that flew arrow-like into the top corner of the Forest goal.

In the 81st minute, the Reds' skilful Welsh defender Terry Hennessey scored with a header from a corner to set-up a barnstorming finish. Forest launched attack-after-attack in the final ten minutes, but Spurs defended desperately and clung on to seal a 2-1 victory. A return to Wembley was their reward.

Tottenham's opponents in the final were to be Jimmy's first club, Chelsea, 1-0 winners over Leeds United in the other semi-final at Villa Park. It was to be the first ever FA Cup final contested by two London clubs.

Tottenham's FA Cup run breathed new life into the team and re-ignited their League campaign. A remarkable run of nine wins and a draw in their last 10 matches saw the

Jim does not look best pleased to have a pint of the sponsors' milk to celebrate Tottenham's 1967 FA Cup final win with team-mate Mike England. Wrong sort of pint!

Lilywhites soar back up the table. But they had left themselves too much to do and finished the season in third position – four points behind Charlton/Best/Law-inspired champions Manchester United and losing out on goal difference to Nottingham Forest in the race for the runners-up spot.

With the League campaign done-and-dusted for another term, Spurs could now concentrate on the end-of-season showpiece – the FA Cup final against Chelsea.

On May 20th 1967, Tottenham and Chelsea lined-up at Wembley in front of 100,000 fans for the 'Cockney Cup final'.

What was to follow was unfortunately, a massive let-down. As so often happens, a much-anticipated Wembley final proved to be a great disappointment. A strangely subdued atmosphere, a torrential second-half downpour and an overpowering sense of a 'fear-of-losing' attitude in both teams, combined to produce a damp-squib of a final with few highlights.

For long periods Jimmy, was expertly man-marked out of the game by Ron Harris. Jim has since told me that the famed-and-feared 'Chopper' was the defender he least liked facing. Ironically, they've always been good mates off the pitch, and now regularly appear together on the stage shows that I promote, reminiscing about the good old days. Jim says that Chopper is a bruise on his memory.

It was left to Jimmy Robertson and Frank Saul to step-up from the supporting cast into starring roles. Masterfully aided by the inspirational Dave Mackay – miraculously back after a second broken leg – and the cool, composed Mike England, they drove Spurs on to Cup glory.

Robertson scored the Tottenham opener just before half-time, pouncing after an Alan Mullery shot had been blocked.

For much of the afternoon, the inexperienced Chelsea team seemed overawed and Spurs found themselves 2-0 ahead midway through the second-half without ever really moving out of third-gear. Man-of-the-match Frank Saul scored Tottenham's second in the 68th minute following a Robertson knock-down from a Mackay long throw.

Tottenham's second goal finally sparked the Blues into life. Scottish entertainer Charlie Cooke – bought by Tommy Docherty as replacement for Tottenham-bound Terry Venables – began to sparkle with his mazy dribbling, finally escaping the shackles of Spurs' baby-faced defender Joe Kinnear.

Five minutes from time, a Bobby Tambling header from a John Boyle cross, brought the scoreline back to 2-1, promising an exciting climax. But it proved to be nothing more than a consolation as Tottenham played comfortable keep-ball as the clock ran down.

And so it was that captain courageous Dave Mackay led his team up the Wembley steps and lifted the FA Cup. Tottenham Hotspur had won another trophy and had also maintained their record of never having lost an FA Cup final.

The 1967 FA Cup-winning team:

Jennings, Kinnear, Knowles, Mullery, England, Mackay (Capt.), Mullery, Robertson, Greaves, Gilzean, Venables, Saul

Jimmy on Tottenham's 1967 FA Cup triumph

❛I have to be honest and admit that we did not produce a particularly memorable final. I believe that one reason the whole match fell a bit flat was because both teams were from London. That robbed the match of much of its atmosphere because the supporters were not in that bubbling 'Oop for the Cup' day-out mood.

Another reason goes deeper into the minds of us mad footballers: By the time a player becomes a professional, it's very rare to find one of us who hasn't played in a losing team in a cup final at some level. There is no worse feeling in the game than losing the big match and, for all Englishmen, the FA Cup final is the biggest of them all.

If you have a stinker and lose a League game, there's always the chance to put things right a few days later. There are no second chances in an FA Cup final, which results in the majority of us playing without our usual freedom and inhibitions – fetch the straitjackets, nurse.

My abiding memory of that afternoon is the performance of our skipper Dave Mackay. He was on a personal mission to win, having been inactive for so long, and he was driving us on like a man possessed.

Everyone involved at Spurs was so pleased for Jimmy Robertson and Frank Saul. They were real unsung heroes of the team who seldom received the praise or recognition they deserved. It was great to see them have their day in the spotlight.❜

For Jimmy, the 1966-67 international season was a case of much ado about very little as Alf Ramsey, quite rightly, allowed his World Cup-winning team an unchanged run.

Jimmy returned for the annual grudge match against Scotland on April 15th 1967. Injuries reduced Ray Wilson, Jack Charlton and Jim to mere passengers as England ended the game with eight fit players.

The Scots celebrated a 3-2 victory, the travelling Tartan Army famously returned home with much of the dug-up Wembley turf and a broken goal as souvenirs and the

Graphic artist Art Turner captures Jimmy on the run during the 1967 FA Cup final, with Chelsea's Scottish defender John Boyle in pursuit.

Scottish press hailed their team as the real world champions. Welcome back, Jim.

In the following international, Jimmy scored his final goal for England in a 2-0 victory over Spain at Wembley. He was to represent England just once more, finishing his England career with 44 goals in 57 England games. The statistics speak for themselves; his strike rate in an England shirt was remarkable.

Jimmy on that defeat by Scotland
'We knew the Scots meant business when Denis Law came out wearing shin pads for the first time any of us could remember. He was ready to run through walls – and his Manchester United team-mate Nobby Stiles – to make an impact, and he scored Scotland's first goal after 28 minutes.

Bobby Lennox and Jim McCalliog also found the net. Jack Charlton, limping at centre-forward, got one back for us, and Geoff Hurst made it 3-2 in a dramatic finish.

There were incredible scenes at the end when the Scottish fans invaded the pitch and started digging up Wembley as if it belonged to them. And about half a dozen of them swung from the crossbar until it snapped.

Only the Jocks could then claim they were the unofficial world champions, ignoring the fact that Jack Charlton, Ray Wilson and I were all limping. We were virtually down to eight players.'

At club level, Jimmy had yet again ended a season as Tottenham's leading goalscorer with 25 – finishing third in the First Division scoring charts, behind Southampton's Ron Davies and West Ham and England hero Geoff Hurst. Add to that his six vital FA Cup goals and you have yet another terrific season for the little genius that was James Peter Greaves.

With his illness and World Cup misery now fading to memory, Jimmy was in a good place. As the Sixties continued to swing – now taking on a psychedelic hue – Spurs, with silverware back in the trophy room, approached the new season in confident mood…

9: *End of the England Road*

THE1967-68 season would prove to be frustrating for both Jimmy and Tottenham. It started with one of the more amusing and amazing goals ever scored, and finished with Jimmy confirmed as an EX-England player.

A thrilling Charity Shield encounter between Spurs and Manchester United at Old Trafford on August 12th got the season off to a flying start. The game has gone down in footballing folklore thanks to a remarkable goal by Pat Jennings, who scored with a 90-yard, wind-assisted clearance that bounced over United goalkeeper Alex Stepney and into the net.

As the bemused Spurs players looked around to see who had scored – they had their backs to to the ball – it suddenly dawned on them that Pat Jennings had found the net. Jimmy turned to Alan Gilzean and said: 'Hey Gilly, do you realise that makes Pat our top scorer?' The game ended in a 3-3 draw and the two teams shared the Shield. It was to be the only silverware seen at The Lane that season.

By Christmas 1967, Tottenham's erratic form saw them sitting mid-table. They had won 10, drawn six and lost eight of their first 24 League games with Jimmy scoring 11 times. This was a more than respectable strike-rate for most mere mortals, but way down on the usual Greaves output. Bill Nicholson decided a shake-up was required.

He made a significant move in the transfer market in January 1968, signing the up-and-coming striker Martin Chivers from Southampton for a then club-record £125,000. The deal involved Frank Saul moving from White Hart Lane to The Dell.

Built like a brick outhouse, 22-year-old Grammar school-educated Chivers was skilful and hungry. Nobody was quite clear whether Bill Nick wanted to play him with the mighty G-Men or in place of one of them.

In the early weeks of the New Year, after a couple of blank Saturdays for Jim, the unthinkable finally happened. Jimmy was dropped for the first time in his Tottenham career. Nicholson decided to pick Chivers and Alan Gilzean up-front leaving no room for Jim – things would never quite be the same again.

There were whispered rumours that Spurs were preparing to sell their once prize asset, much to the undisguised annoyance of Spurs fans (like me) who never wanted to see Jim playing in another club's colours.

Brash Derby manager Brian Clough was sniffing around, and there was also interest at Manchester City and West Ham. But Bill Nick quashed the transfer talk by recalling

Jim for a fourth round FA Cup tie against Preston North End at White Hart Lane.

Steve Richards reported in *The Sun* of February 19th 1968, the day before Jimmy's 28th birthday:

> 'Jimmy Greaves, the master executioner, gave a two-goal answer to those people who thought he had lost his scoring appetite. He knocked Preston out of the FA Cup to finally kill off talk that Spurs would even consider parting with one of the game's true artists. There have been rumblings and rumours all week that Tottenham will be prepared to let Greaves go if they get the right offer, but when I put this to Bill Nicholson he dismissed it as idle gossip with no basis in truth. I have been watching Greaves since his first kick in club football, and he may have lost a yard in speed since his hepatitis illness of 1965, but he remains the finest and sharpest finisher in the First Division. I think there would be an uprising of Spurs supporters if Tottenham even contemplated selling him.'

Tottenham won the tie against Preston 3-1, with Chivers scoring their other goal. The dreams of a return to Wembley were dashed in the next round when Spurs were beaten 2-1 by Liverpool in a fifth round replay at Anfield.

Inconsistency continued to blight Tottenham's League campaign until they hit a purple patch in March with four straight wins. They beat Stoke 3-0, followed by 5-0 and 6-1 wallopings of Burnley and Southampton – Jimmy scoring twice in each of the latter games.

The winning streak reached a climax with a 2-1 victory over Leeds United at The Lane on April 12th 1968. Peter Batt reported in *The Sun*:

> 'Leeds, the team that had forgotten how to lose, yesterday received a rude reminder from Spurs about the despair of defeat. It was their first set-back in 27 matches and, almost inevitably, it was that genius of a goalscorer Jimmy Greaves who conjured up the winning goal. How and why Greaves is not a regular member of Ramsey's England squad is a complete mystery to me. His would be the first name on my team sheet, but we all know that Alf has always suffered from Greaves blindness.'

The wayward form returned, and Spurs managed just two wins in their final seven League games of the season – despite Jimmy finding the back of the net five times in the last five fixtures.

Jimmy was never famous for his heading, but here's proof that he was willing to try. He is challenging Arsenal goalkeeper Jim 'Fingers' Furnell. Looking on are Gunners George Armstrong and Ian Ure, and that's Martin Chivers in the No 9 Spurs shirt.

A far from vintage First Division campaign had ended with Spurs in seventh place – 11 points behind champions Manchester City, masterminded by Joe Mercer and Malcolm Allison and featuring the quality trio Mike Summerbee, Colin Bell and Francis Lee. Joe Mercer made no secret of the fact that he would also have liked Jimmy Greaves in his attack.

Jimmy's late goal spree had taken his season's haul to 23. Yet again, he was comfortably Tottenham's top scorer.

Fleet Street started a campaign to get Greaves recalled to the England team, and Alf Ramsey – now Sir Alf – startled the press in general and Jimmy in particular when he announced in unusually stark terms: "I am being crucified because I have not brought Greaves back into the squad. I feel I should let it be known publicly that Jimmy has asked me not to consider him again for England."

Jimmy on the end of his international career

'Little did I know at the time, that a meaningless friendly in Vienna was to be my last outing in an England shirt. One damaging misquote haunted me for much of my career, and then an honest comment led to a misunderstanding with Alf Ramsey and resulted in the end of my England days.

Firstly, early in my career it was claimed that I had said that I 'had no fire in my belly' when playing for England. I never uttered those words but they appeared in print and many people took them as gospel and thought I played with less than total commitment when on international duty. I promise you I always gave my best for England and can point to 44 goals in 57 matches as my evidence – but that false statement was continually brought out and dogged me throughout my career.

What I had said to Alf during my last training session with his squad at Roehampton was that I would rather not be called up unless I was going to play. When the press campaign for my recall gathered pace, I was astonished when Alf said I had told him that I didn't want to play for England.

Alf completely misunderstood me if he really did believe that I had asked him not to select me anymore. I still wanted to represent my country, I was just frustrated at being included in the training squads and then not playing in the matches. What I said to Alf was, "Please do not call me up if you do not intend to play me," which is very different from saying I did not wish to be considered for England again. Let's face it, I was never the most enthusiastic of trainers and being a peripheral member of the squad did not appeal to me. I was just being honest with Alf, and he misunderstood.'

With another new campaign on the horizon, Jimmy – now a former England international – trained hard and primed himself for what would prove one last truly prolific season as a Spurs player…

10: An Indian Summer in N17

DESPITE the positive tones of this Indian Summer chapter heading, Tottenham made a disastrous start to the 1968-69 season. An opening day 2-1 home defeat to bitter rivals Arsenal understandably knocked the confidence of the players. In the following weeks, palpable feelings of frustration and apprehension hit both team and supporters alike, spreading like bushfire in a drought.

The exception to the rule was, inevitably, Jimmy. He began the new campaign in majestic form. While Spurs won just one of their first six League matches – losing three and drawing two – a recharged and rejuvenated Jim was on target in four of those opening encounters. It was a sign of things to come.

The rest of the team at last burst into life in a dramatic afternoon at The Lane on September 7th 1968. The victims were the 'Clarets' of Burnley and their main tormentor was, of course, Jimmy. The performance that kick-started Tottenham's season was witnessed by Peter Corrigan of the *Daily Mail*:

> •It is like welcoming back an old friend to see Jimmy Greaves thieving goals with his old panache. He helped himself to a hat-trick and created three other goals in this 7-0 blitz of Burnley.•

Two wins and two draws followed as Spurs steadily climbed the table from the lowly depths of the First Division.

Leicester City were next to visit White Hart Lane on October 5th. Jimmy helped himself to yet another hat-trick – with one of his goals certainly making an impression with the Tottenham boss. Brian Scovell wrote in the *Daily Sketch*:

> •Manager Bill Nicholson described the first of Jimmy Greaves's three goals against Leicester as possibly the greatest he has ever scored. He collected a clearance from Pat Jennings, beat four men in a 30-yard run and finished it with a perfectly-placed left foot shot.•

Two weeks later Jimmy was on target again, scoring both Tottenham goals in a 2-1 victory over Liverpool at White Hart Lane. One of the goals was hilarious, as Jimmy and Terry Venables played a classic three-card trick on bemused Liverpool defenders. The two cheeky Cockneys pulled off a fast one that would have made Arthur Daley and Del-Boy proud. Harry Miller reported in the *Daily Mirror*.

'Liverpool's defenders had eyes only for Terry Venables as he feigned anger at the positioning of their defensive wall. Greaves stepped up unnoticed and cheekily curled his 199th First Division goal for Tottenham into the net.'

Jimmy on the business of goals

'I've never been one to get overly excited about the quality of goals. I was just happy as long as they crossed the line. A toe-poke in a goalmouth scramble was just as important to me as one of my more elaborate efforts. It doesn't matter how they get there as long as they count as goals. Cheeky goals always gave me a lot of satisfaction. I always liked to play off the cuff and when it came off like the Venners free-kick routine we knew we were providing terrific entertainment.

My personal favourite in the cheeky category was a penalty I took against Gordon Banks in a match between Spurs and Leicester. As I bent down to put the ball on the spot I noticed Gordon going through his usual pre-penalty ritual of spitting on his hands and reaching for a post to get his distance. He had his left arm stretched out and was looking at the post when, still crouched at the penalty spot, I rolled the ball ever so gently with my left foot into the opposite corner of the net. It was part joke and part me thinking 'I wonder if I'll get away with this?' I fully expected the kick to be taken again but went through the pretence of celebrating. I don't know who was more shocked, Gordon or me, when the ref awarded a goal. Just to rub it in Gordon got booked for protesting!'

As the season progressed, Jimmy continued to score seemngly at will and the media campaign calling for his return to the England team gathered momentum. On November 16th, Jimmy produced a sublime performance against Sunderland at The Lane. Vic Railton of the *Evening News* reported:

'Jimmy Greaves snatched four goals in this 5-1 slamming of Sunderland. How much longer can England afford to ignore the claims of Britain's top hot-shot? Jinking Jimmy might easily have had at least another two goals as he ran the Sunderland defence ragged.'

A Jimmy riddle .. what do you think Greavsie and Terry Venables are discussing so intently? Politics? Where to meet for a drink after the match? Answer: They are inspecting the Wembley pitch before the 1967 FA Cup final against Chelsea.

There was a sudden dip in the Tottenham League form and they endured a harsh Christmas – failing to win in six matches from late November. Spurs faced a New Year out of the title race but, with cup football suiting their style, there was still much to play for.

During this year, and worthy of honourable mention, 1968 saw the departure of two Lane legends – Dave Mackay and Cliff Jones. The mighty Mackay joined Derby County, where he was to further his legend by winning League titles – first as player and then manager. Flying Welsh winger Cliff Jones, the supplier of so many of Jim's goals, joined Fulham after 10 years distinguished years at Spurs.

The last two remaining members of the great Double team had left The Lane – Another era-defining moment in Spurs history.

Let's get back to the Tottenham cup campaigns of 1968-69. In the second round of the League Cup, Spurs beat Aston Villa 4-1 at Villa Park with Martin Chivers scoring a hat-trick. In the next round against Exeter City at The Lane, it was Jimmy who helped himself to three goals in a 6-3 smashing of The Grecians. Jim scored the only goal of the fourth round tie against Peterborough and Peter Collins booked Spurs a semi-final place with the winning goal against Southampton in the next round.

Arsenal were Tottenham's opponents in a tense two-legged semi-final. An injury-time John Radford goal gave Arsenal a precious 1-0 win in a tight first-leg at Highbury on November 20th 1968. In the second-leg at The Lane two weeks later, Jimmy was on target to level the tie but another late Radford goal, in an often brutal encounter, made it 2-1 on aggregate and took the game beyond Spurs. Arsenal's delight ended in despair, when they went down in the final to Third Division Swindon Town.

Tottenham's FA Cup quest began with a tricky third round tie at Walsall in which Jimmy scored the only goal of the game. He was on the scoresheet again in the fourth round 2-1 win over Wolves. In the fifth round Spurs took on Aston Villa at White Hart Lane on February 12th 1969. Desmond Hackett, of the *Daily Express*, reported:

> •Rejected by goal-bankrupt England, Jimmy Greaves scored twice to put Tottenham into the sixth round of the FA Cup last night at the expense of Tommy Docherty's Aston Villa braves. The magical Greaves was the difference between two evenly matched sides in a 3-2 victory that had the dejected Doc looking in need of a doc.•

A crowd of 48,000 saw eventual FA Cup-winners Manchester City dash Tottenham's Cup dreams in the quarter-final at Maine Road on March 1st 1969. City won the match 1-0 with a Francis Lee goal separating the teams in an open match that was a credit to two truly entertaining sides.

Tottenham regrouped and put their cup disappointment behind them, winning four League matches in April. They recorded wins against Coventry, Nottingham Forest, West Ham and Southampton, with Jimmy scoring five goals that month.

Spurs ended the season sixth in the table, 22 points behind champions Leeds United. With 27 League goals, Jim was the First Division's leading scorer for an incredible sixth-time in his career. In all competitions, Jimmy scored 36 goals in 52 matches for Tottenham in the 1968-69 season. What a player.

As the wild and wonderful decade that was the Sixties drew to a close, Jimmy was approaching 30 but was in prolific form and great shape. There was little indication that his Tottenham journey was about to hit rocky roads.

Jimmy on the Swinging Sixties

'They say if you can remember the Sixties, you weren't there. Well I can remember them and can tell you that they were what you might call a rather eventful decade for me. At the start I was at Chelsea, then had my unhappy experience in Italy before the best football days of my life with Tottenham, There were the contrasting World Cups of 1962 and 1966, and I don't think I am giving away any secrets when I say the finals staged in England gave me my greatest disappointment in football. But all in all, the Sixties were memorable and, yes, I guess they swung for much of the time

.What I do know is the football we played in that decade was more entertaining and value-for-money for the spectators than a lot of the stuff served up today. It was a game of physical contact – an understatement when you think of defenders like Chopper Harris, Bites Yer Legs Hunter and Iron Tommy Smith. Nowadays, if you breathe on a forward he invariably collapses as if he's been shot. I wonder how Drogba, a fine player who goes over too easily, would have fared against Billy Bremner coming at him with a two-footed challenge?

We were not aloof from our public back then, while today's players disappear behind their security fences and have little or no contact with fans and reporters. Many of the journalists 'in my day' were and remain my best mates. Now the media can't get near the so-called stars because of a fortress put up by their agents.'

THE 1969-70 season began as the last had ended, with Jimmy in fine form and Spurs inconsistent. He scored in the two opening fixtures – a 3-1 defeat at Leeds and a 4-0 victory over Burnley. There was no indication that this would prove Jimmy's last season at White Hart Lane, where he was an icon idolised by the Tottenham faithful. I followed his career avidly, and it never entered my head that he could play for any other team but Spurs.

On August 30th, Jimmy reached another milestone with Spurs, as Bob Ferrier reported in the *Sunday Express*:

> 'A peerless, vintage goal to crown a great occasion. It came from the one and only Jimmy Greaves as he celebrated his 300th League game for Spurs. He found the Ipswich net with an incredible over-head flick with his left foot.'

Having made an adequate start to the season, the following six weeks saw Tottenham's form dip alarmingly and Jimmy's goals dried up.

The really good days were now few and far between but all the more memorable when they arrived. Such was the case when Newcastle visited White Hart Lane on October 18th. Jimmy scored both goals in a 2-1 win, one of which had Peter Corrigan of the *Daily Mail* eulogising:

> 'It was a goal fashioned out of nothing. Greaves collected the ball five yards inside his own half and then set off on an extraordinary 60-yard gallop at the end of which the ball was tucked into the back of the Newcastle net and a queue of beaten defenders were left fighting for breath.'

At the end of the year, Jimmy's contribution to football in the Sixties was recognised by the men who knew the most. The *Daily Express* conducted a poll among the League managers: "Jimmy Greaves was voted their top striker of the Sixties by the managers who were in power during the greatest decade in the history of English football. Greaves pipped Geoff Hurst, with Francis Lee edging Denis Law into fourth place."

As the Sixties made way for the Seventies, it was rough sailing on the good ship Spurs. They sat mid-table and were not playing well. Many in football, including Bill Nicholson, also began to question Jim's commitment to the game.

The new decade began with Jimmy scoring three goals in a replayed FA Cup third round tie against Bradford City. In the following League game against Derby County at White Hart Lane on January 10th 1970, Jimmy scored his final goal for Tottenham Hotspur in a 2-1 victory.

It was to be an FA Cup tie that would hasten Jimmy's departure from Tottenham. Following a 0-0 draw at The Lane, Spurs travelled to Selhurst Park to face Crystal Palace in an FA Cup fourth round replay on January 28th. A game that provided the headline-writers with A-grade material was to be Jimmy's last ever match for Tottenham Hotspur. Gerry Queen scored the goal that knocked Spurs out of the FA Cup – can you guess where this is going? The most imaginative headline on the back-pages of the following day's newspapers read: 'QUEEN WINS THE GAME FOR PALACE!'

Bill Nicholson lost patience and axed half his team for the next League game against Southampton. Among the casualties were Cyril Knowles, Alan Gilzean and Jimmy, who was never to return to the first-team.

For several weeks Jimmy's career came to a standstill and he spent more time on motor rally trial runs than he did on football matters. Jim had accepted an offer from the Ford Motor Company to join their team for the 1970 *Daily Mirror* sponsored World Cup rally to Mexico. As with all things in his life, Jimmy wanted to do it well and trained hard under the tutelage of his co-driver Tony Fall. Bill Nick read Jim's interest in four wheels rather than a football as a sign that he was losing his appetite for the game. Following a meeting to end the stalemate, it was clear that Jimmy didn't feature in Bill Nick's current first-team plans and he agreed to think about letting Jim move on – but nothing definite was decided.

As transfer-deadline day approached, Derby County and Manchester City had been among clubs showing an interest in Jim. Then, on March 16th – deadline day itself – Jim received a phone call from Bill Nicholson telling him to get himself down to Upton Park. By the end of the day Jimmy was a West Ham player. A record £200,000 transfer deal saw Martin Peters join Tottenham, with Jimmy moving the other way as a £54,000 makeweight.

After nine glorious years, Jim reluctantly said goodbye to White Hart Lane. He had scored a never-to-be-beaten club record 220 League goals for Spurs in 321 matches. In all competitive first-team football with Spurs Jim scored 307 goals in 420 games.

Any Spurs fan who doesn't include Jimmy in their Tottenham all-time XI obviously never saw the little genius at the peak of his powers. He was untouchable.

Jimmy on his reasons for joining West Ham

'I knew I could have done a lot better financally because I'd had several tasty offers made on the old hush-hush while I was out of the Tottenham team. But the thought of joining Mooro and Geoff Hurst and the fact that the Hammers training ground was just a fifteen-minute drive from my home and businesses lulled me into a signing that I have regretted ever since. Looking back on that day, I just wish I had told Bill Nick that I was not interested. He would still have completed the signing of Martin from West Ham because the £54,000 valuation put on me as a makeweight in the deal was chickenfeed to Spurs. But I had been so switched off from football that I was not thinking straight and agreed to join West Ham. It seemed such a convenient move at the time.'

At the time of Jim's arrival at Upton Park, West Ham were 17th in the First Division and in danger of getting sucked into a relegation battle with the five teams below them – Ipswich Town, Southampton, Crystal Palace, Sunderland and Sheffield Wednesday.

The West Ham squad of that time was full of talent, with legends Bobby Moore and Geoff Hurst alongside players of the calibre of Billy Bonds, Frank Lampard Snr, Ronnie Boyce, Harry Redknapp, Clyde Best, John Sissons and a young Trevor Brooking.

On a good day, they were sublime and the whole of Upton Park would bubble. In the best West Ham traditions, they played to entertain. Consistency, however, was not one of their strengths. On a bad day, they'd ship four or five whilst trying in vain to create the perfect goal at the other end.

But on the 'social' side, they were far more consistent. As on the pitch, Bobby Moore was the captain – leading a formidable drinking school including regulars John Cushley, Brian Dear, Frank Lampard, John Charles, Harry Redknapp, Jimmy Lindsay and occasionally, Geoff Hurst – Jim quickly fitted into his new role as trusted lieutenant at the side of captain Moore. Jim and Mooro always roomed together on England trips and were close pals. They had famously danced together on the pitch during a Tottenham visit to West Ham in an era when there was still fun in football. Now they had plenty of time to drink togeher.

Jimmy had been a leading member of the Dave Mackay drinking school at Tottenham. Now he was a regular at Bobby Moore's side as they sunk pints galore. Bobby was famous for having hollow legs, while the drink was taking a hold on Jimmy without him being aware of it until it was too late.

On March 21st 1970, five days after becoming a Hammer, Jimmy made his West

Who would have believed it – Jimmy and Geoff together in West Ham shirts

Ham debut in the League match against Manchester City at Maine Road. It could only end one way. Alan Hoby reported in the *Sunday Express*:

> •Jimmy Greaves – greatest goalscorer of our time, perhaps of all time – has done it again. In a bizarre and fantastic game against Manchester City, our Jim launched West Ham to a 5-1 victory – their biggest win of the season – with two typical cool and cheeky goals. He has now scored in all his major debuts.•

The West Ham line-up: Grotier, Bonds, Lampard, Boyce, Stephenson, Moore (capt.), Holland, Eustace (Llewellyn), Hurst, Greaves, Howe

At this point, please allow me put together the facts of the 'Greaves Debut Phenomenon' into one easy-to-swallow paragraph. It deserves to be read, possibly learnt word-for-word and could even be used as a meditative mantra:

> Jimmy played his first League game for Chelsea against Tottenham at White Hart Lane on August 23rd 1957 – and scored. He made his debut for England Under-23s against Bulgaria at Stamford Bridge on September 25th 1957 – and scored twice. He made his full international debut for England against Peru in Lima on May 17th 1959 – and scored. He made his debut for AC Milan against Botafogo at the San Siro on June 7th 1961 – and scored. He made his debut for Tottenham against Blackpool at White Hart Lane on December 16th 1961 – and scored a hat-trick. He played in his first FA Cup final for Spurs against Burnley at Wembley on May 5th 1962 – and scored. He made his debut for West Ham against Manchester City at Maine Road on March 21st 1970 – and scored two goals.

They always talk about making a good first impression. Jim did it wherever he went, and still does it, wherever he goes. In a word? Remarkable.

West Ham followed-up the impressive victory over Manchester City with an away draw at Crystal Palace and a home win over Liverpool. Their First Division safety was guaranteed in the game against Wolves at Upton Park on March 31st, with goals from Jimmy, Billy Bonds and Bobby Howe contributing to a 3-0 West Ham win. A 2-2 draw against Leeds and a 2-1 defeat at Arsenal – with Jimmy scoring the West Ham consolation – brought the Hammers' season to a close in relatively positive fashion.

They finished 17th in the table and, with Jimmy playing a vital role, had comfortably avoided relegation. Since joining the club, Jim had scored four goals in six League games as the Hammers won three and drew two of his first half-dozen matches as a West Ham player. It was not startling, but it was satisfactory.

The fact that these six matches were played in a hectic two-week schedule could mean only one thing – it was World Cup year. The 1970 finals were to kick-off in Mexico City on May 31st. With no place in the England squad for the finals, Jimmy still headed for Mexico – in a rally car...

When asked what have been the toughest challenges he has faced in his life, Jimmy will answer: 'Apart from trying to give up drink, it would have to be driving in the 1970 World Cup rally.'

A cluster of 96 cars left Wembley Stadium to drive 16,245 miles. Only 23 cars completed the marathon challenge. Tony Fall and Jimmy, in their battered black-and-white Ford Escort, not only completed the race but managed to finish in a commendable sixth place.

Along the way they suffered eleven punctures, a damaged suspension and a broken half-shaft. They had witnessed the aftermath of an earthquake in Peru and landslides in Ecuador. They narrowly avoided death when swerving to avoid an old peasant lady on a mountain road, their car skidding to a halt, just inches from a sheer drop. On a pitch-black winding road in Panama, their car collided with a galloping horse splattering a shaken Jimmy and Tony in broken glass and blood. It was some adventure.

Jimmy on the 1970 World Cup rally
'If I had realised how hard the race was going to be I doubt if I could have summoned up the courage to face it. We used to go 55 hours in one stretch without sleep as we navigated the toughest terrain in the world, driving at speeds of up to 100mph. on mountain roads that were built with only donkey transport in mind. Those rally drivers are among the toughest and most fearless sportsmen I have ever met. There were times when I felt physically sick over the demands of the race and several times wanted to quit but there was no way I could let Tony Fall down.'

Jimmy arrived in Mexico City just 24 hours after Bobby Moore had flown in from Bogota following his infamous arrest on a trumped-up jewel theft charge.

Bobby had been hidden away from the world's Press in an Embassy house on the outskirts of the city. Knowing that Mooro would welcome the company of some old drinking pals after his harrowing experience Jim – with Bobby's business associate Lou Wade in tow – decided to pay him a visit.

As they arrived at the embassy house in a taxi Lou – 6ft 7in tall and garishly dressed

– provided a spectacular distraction to the gathered journalists, newsmen, cameramen and security guards while Jim sneaked round the back, over the wall and through some French windows. Just as he caught sight of Bobby, Jim was asked to leave by the embassy official's enraged wife. Bobby later said: 'There I was in the back of beyond having not seen a familiar face for days, and suddenly Jimmy Greaves is in front of me, being escorted to the door while receiving a severe ear-bashing. I just stood there open-mouthed and speechless, trying and failing to make sense of what I was seeing.'

After much apologising and negotiation Jimmy and Lou Wade were allowed in to see Bobby. The first question Jimmy asked him was 'What did you do with the bracelet, Mooro?' The embassy wife was speechless. Jimmy's humour was lost on her and he might have been from another planet as far as she was concerned. And standing next to him, Lou Wade in his canary yellow jacket, thick-rimmed glasses and towering above everybody, his head almost hitting the chandeliers dripping from the ceiling. She excused herself and left the room, wondering what on earth the ambassador would make of it all.

Beginning to appreciate the surreal hilarity of their situation and, with the embassy drinks cabinet within easy reach, the trio enjoyed a relaxing night. Mission accomplished.

Bobby and Jim went their separate ways. Jimmy flew off to the West Indies for a holiday with Irene. Mooro led a strong and confident England squad into the World Cup. Abiding memories for England, in what was the greatest of all World Cups, were a 1-0 defeat to the great Brazilians in a classic encounter and including the stupendous 'Save of the Century' by Gordon Banks from Pelé, which we have immortalised in print (*Banks v Pelé*, www.a1sportingmemorabilia.co.uk), and then the heartbreaking extra-time defeat to West Germany in the quarter-finals. If Gordon had been fit to play and had Alf Ramsey more experience in the use of substitutes, who knows what might have happened?

With a new season on the horizon at West Ham, sun-tanned Jimmy headed home after his holiday to prepare – but something was missing. For the first time in his footballing life there was no excitement or butterflies as a season approached. In hindsight, you could say that in the previous couple of years, there had been early signs of a growing disinterest in the game. But now it was definite – Jimmy, a busy businessman and heavy social drinker, had lost his appetite for football and a decision had to be made…

 # 12: *The Blackpool Affair and Retirement*

WITH his heart committed, but his drive and enthusiasm at an all-time low, Jimmy and his beleaguered West Ham colleagues gathered for another new season. The fixture list had served up a fascinating schedule, with West Ham having to face three fierce local derbies in each of their first three matches of the new term.

Considering his mindset, matches against Tottenham, Arsenal and Chelsea in the space of the first week of the new campaign must have been, at the very least, thought provoking and poignant for Jim.

On the opening day of the League season, Jim received the welcome of a homecoming-hero at White Hart Lane as West Ham visited Spurs on August 15th 1970. I'm sure that even the most partisan Spurs fan would have been inwardly delighted to see Jim score in a 2-2 draw. A point earned in each of the two following all-London affairs saw West Ham sitting mid-table, having drawn their three first three League games. That was about as good as it got.

Of their next eight matches, West Ham lost four, drew three and won just one with an increasingly disillusioned Jimmy failing to find the net. In mid-September Ron Greenwood told Bobby Moore and Jimmy that he was considering resigning. The initial Greaves reaction was of the 'if he goes I go' variety. The thought of making an escape from West Ham was now prevalent in Jimmy's mind.

Jim finally returned to scoring ways in a 2-1 defeat to Stoke at the Victoria Ground on October 10th. Further goals against Blackpool, Derby and Liverpool before the end of the year did little to improve the confidence of Jim or the team as West Ham finished 1970 just one place above the relegation zone. They had won just three of their first 22 League games of the season.

Despite their plight and the stuttering Greaves form, no one at Upton Park – least of all Jim – could have possibly foreseen how quickly the relationship would deteriorate into the untenable.

A seemingly innocent night-out in the New Year of 1971, was to grow into a headline-hitting controversy that would quickly become the unstoppable force that was to end the professional playing career of Jimmy Greaves.

On the frozen New Year's Day of 1971, Spurs travelled to Blackpool for an FA Cup third round tie to be played the following afternoon at Bloomfield Road. After a couple of drinks at their Imperial Hotel base, Jimmy and Bobby Moore were heading for an early night when a chance encounter with a couple of BBC *Match of the Day* cameramen led to a furore that was to feature on the front and back pages of the national press for weeks to come.

One of the cameramen informed Bobby and Jim that the Blackpool pitch was iced over and that 'it will be a miracle if it's fit for play.' Within minutes, Messrs. Moore and Greaves, an eager Brian Dear and curious teetotaller Clyde Best were in a taxi heading for ex-boxer Brian London's 007 nightclub. Less than three hours later, without incident and hardly the worse for wear, the players were safely back at their hotel – but they had been spotted.

As so often happens, when you least want it to, the 'miracle' duly occurred. The tie went ahead and, on a pitch resembling a skating rink, Blackpool beat West Ham 4-0. Step forward the 'spotter.' An irate Hammers fan who had seen four players drinking in the 007 the night before the match, telephoned the club and a newspaper to complain. With a little journalistic tweaking, a full-blown scandal was born.

The scapegoats had been identified and singled out, but it was the way they were hung out to dry that proved to be the final straw for Jim. West Ham waited until the day after Bobby Moore had been captured by Eamonn Andrews and his *This Is Your Life* red book, and then came down on Mooro and Jim like a bucketful of claret-and-blue gunge.

 **Jimmy on the Blackpool Affair**
⁶I made up my mind to retire from football after the incident in Blackpool which was blown up out of all proportion by the media. I was sickened and disgusted by the way the West Ham board – in particular Ron Greenwood – handled the situation. They fined us and dropped us and did it in the full glare of publicity. The story was plastered all over the front pages as if we had been guilty of the crime of the century. We deserved to have disciplinary action taken against us but it could easily have been done privately. I was particularly nauseated by the treatment Bobby Moore received. No player has given more loyal service – and top-quality service, at that – than Bobby did to West Ham. But just one step out of line and they cut his legs off. I was disgusted that Alf Ramsey saw fit to drop Bobby for one match.

I had always promised myself that the moment I stopped enjoying my football I would quickly hang up my boots and, from the start of that 1970-71 season, I was thoroughly miserable about West Ham's game and my contribution to it. The so-called Blackpool Affair was the tipping point.⁹

It's the Monday after England's goalless draw with Uruguay in the opening match of the 1966 World Cup. Jimmy and Bobby Moore share a drink and a laugh with Sean Connery and Yul Brynner during a trip to Pinewood Studios. Alf Ramsey thanked "Seen" Connery for his hospitality; Mooro whispered to Greavsie: "That's the funniest thing I've ever shawn or heard."

With Jimmy dropped, disgruntled and disillusioned, West Ham began 1971 with three League defeats sinking them deeper into the relegation mire. He returned, as always, with a winning goal. The victims this time were Coventry City at Highfield Road on February 8th. Bernard Joy of the *Evening Standard* wrote:

> 'With the goal that defeated Coventry, West Ham and former England ace scorer Jimmy Greaves began his reparations for the Blackpool escapade which led to the disciplining of Bobby Moore, Brian Dear, Clyde Best and himself. It was his 353rd League goal and one of his most valuable, considerably easing West Ham's fears of relegation.'

There was still life in the not-so-old-dog yet, as he proved by scoring both West Ham goals against Ipswich Town in a 2-2 draw at Upton Park on March 20th. Bolstered by Jimmy's goals, the Hammers hit their best form of the season and guaranteed their First Division status with three straight wins. Ultimately, it would be the giant names of Blackpool and Burnley facing a future of Second Division football.

The last of those three wins was to prove a final memorable landmark in the career of Jimmy Greaves as he scored his 357th and last ever League goal in West Ham's home game against West Bromwich Albion on April 9th 1971.

Jimmy's mate Norman Giller, who knew he was thinking of quitting and tried to talk him out of it as they collaborated on a book with Reg Gutteridge called *Let's Be Honest*, was there to report the match for the *Daily Express*:

> 'The Jimmy Greaves gift for scoring the goals that really count has rarely been more gratefully accepted than by West Ham at Upton Park. Greaves, as nimble as a thimble, stitched this game up for the Hammers five minutes from the end to leave West Bromwich Albion dazed and dismayed. He steered the ball home from a tight angle after a Brooking shot had been blocked.'

The other West Ham goal that day in a 2-1 win was provided by Bryan 'Pop' Robson, who had joined the Hammers from Newcastle just two months earlier. It was a significant signing. With Geoff Hurst guaranteed his place as first-choice striker, Jim now had to battle with Robson and Clyde Best for the second forward role.

Two wins, a draw and two losses in their following five League games meant that, with their safety assured, West Ham's final match of the season was a meaningless affair against Huddersfield Town at Upton Park on May 1st 1971.

Unknowlingly, a crowd of 24,983 was watching Jimmy Greaves play his last ever professional football match. It was still a secret known only to Jimmy and a small band of close friends and family. For the record, Huddersfield winger Jimmy Lawson scored the only goal of a low-key encounter that will be remembered only for the fact that it featured the final League appearance of arguably the greatest English goalscorer ever to tie a pair of boot laces. The West Ham team:

Ferguson, McDowell, Lampard, Stephenson, Taylor, Moore (Capt.), Redknapp, Bonds, Hurst, Robson, Greaves

And that was that. Jimmy quietly walked away from the game that had been his life with little hullabaloo or fanfare.

At that time, Jim had no regrets. He had several business interests outside of football to keep him occupied and he would no longer have to endure the day-to-day training sessions he had grown to despise.

West Ham had scraped to First Division safety, finishing in 20th place (these were the days when only the bottom two teams were relegated), and Jimmy ended his final season with nine goals in 32 League appearances for the Hammers.

At the ridiculously early age of 31 – leaving an astonishing legacy of 357 League goals in 516 Football League matches and 44 goals in 57 England appearances – James Peter Greaves optimistically stepped into a new life without football. Jimmy's pal Norman Giller was moved to mark his retirement with a poem:

> *Jimmy Greaves*
> *Always pleased us with goals scored with ease*
> *Defenders teased and brought to their knees*
> *Left like scattered leaves by his expertise*
> *Jimmy Greaves*
> *It was as easy for Greavsie as shelling peas*
> *Goals often in threes, goalies left wooden as trees*
> *And drowning in seas as he skimmed by as if on skis*
> *Jimmy Greaves*
> *For him it was just a breeze, natural as honey for bees*
> *Unlocking without keys, an acrobat on the trapeze*
> *Confounding referees, giving us memories that freeze*
> *Jimmy Greaves*

But little was rhyming for Jimmy off the pitch. He had started leaning too heavily on the bottle in low moments and was about to face the biggest battle of his life. Those close to him worried that he had no chance of winning it.

13: *The Fall and Rise of an Idol*

A S I approach this chapter that covers the much-publicised and self-inflicted hiccup in Jimmy's life, I should make it clear that it is fortunate for all of us that this book is not an autobiography. If that were the case, and it was left to Jim to tell his own story, the following pages would be almost completely blank.

The majority of the Seventies passed Jimmy by – with him largely and regrettably incapable of taking part. It is only through the testimony of the friends and family whose love and care helped him through his darkest days, that we can piece together the movements of Jim through his lost years.

At the time of his retirement from football, Jimmy was busy and financially secure. The box-and-packaging business he had started with his brother-in-law, Tom Barden, on his return from Milan had mushroomed into a small but flourishing empire. Other business interests included a country club, sport goods shops, a transport firm, insurance and travel agencies and ladies and menswear shops. Jimmy was chairman of the parent company – a role that often involved taking prospective clients out to eat and, of course, drink.

Jimmy on his new freedom

•When I retired from football at the age of 31, I was suddenly like a prisoner let out of jail. I was free of all the discipline of the last 16 years. No more training. No more do-this-do-that. No more curfews. It was like paradise. Only now, looking back, can I see that it was a fool's paradise. And I was the bloody fool.•

For 18 months after quitting West Ham, Jim didn't touch a football or go near a football ground. His brief return to the big-time was an emotional and memorable night that merits special mention. On October 17th 1972, Jimmy became the first former Tottenham player to have a testimonial match at White Hart Lane. Captain for the day, Greaves led out a Spurs team to face Dutch giants Feyenoord in front of 45,799 spectators. Just three minutes into the game, Jimmy turned back the years and scored a trademark poacher's goal sending the crowd into raptures. It may have been an exhibition but his goal was no gimme. The old magic was still there. Spurs went on to win 2-1 and Jimmy walked away with £22,000. I was there, watching my hero, and I don't mind admitting that I had tears in my eyes through much of the game.

Jimmy was already into his secret drinking binges when this photograph was taken in 1972 following the publication of his Let's Be Honest *book that he wrote in collaboration with Reg Gutteridge (right) and Norman Giller, who says: "It should have been called Let's Be Dishonest, because there was no mention of heavy drinking. That came in our next book together six years later,* This One's On Me."

To this day, Jimmy is still immensely proud that so many fans turned out to give him their support and he will tell you that not a penny of the money was spent on booze. Jim used £12,000 to become a member of Lloyd's Underwriters and spent the rest on home improvements.

As his drinking began to spiral out of control, Jimmy and Irene decided that football – at any level – could possibly provide a cure. He made a return with his local Brentwood team and later with Chelmsford. With Jimmy not in the best of condition, and countless Sunday morning cloggers keen to have the scalp of Jimmy Greaves on their CV, it proved an unsatisfying and short-lived comeback.

The next couple of years saw Jim descend the depths that any recovering alcoholic will recognise only too well. Weeks, sometimes even months, of sobriety were followed by massive benders as he battled his inner demons.

Amazingly, Jim still managed to perform his footballing magic in testimonial and charity games. Keith Burkinshaw and Bill Nicholson were so impressed by his display for Spurs in a Pat Jennings testimonial match at White Hart Lane that they offered him the lifeline of a comeback with Tottenham. Jim went as far as discussing the possibility of a return to Spurs with PFA chairman Derek Dougan. Eventually, with Jimmy's confidence at an all-time low and afraid of possibly letting down his beloved Tottenham, the plans were abandoned. Around this time, Jim also sold out his interests in the company he and Tom had so proudly and conscientiously built up over the years. Left with a couple of menswear shops – which inevitably went bust – and a travel agency, Jim continued on his descent towards rock bottom.

Jimmy on his alcoholism

'The last person who wants to recognise the symptoms of alcoholism is the alcoholic. For two years I did my best to kid myself that drink had not become a problem. I would pack it up after the next session. I'd tell myself, 'next week, Jimbo, you will go on the wagon. Start getting fit again. Play a bit of squash, some golf and maybe join a Sunday team. I'm only 34. I'll pack up drinking and play a lot of sport. Starting next week.'

Of course, next week never came. I did start playing a lot of sport. Golf, squash, tennis and the occasional charity and Sunday match. But the drinking continued and being physically fit meant I had a faster recovery rate after my heavy sessions than most alcoholics. People would see me competing at sport and never believe that they were watching somebody who within the past 48 hours had knocked back two bottles of vodka and a couple of gallons of beer.'

With the wonderful Irene and the kids unable to watch the husband and Dad they loved so much destroy himself, it was agreed that Jimmy should move out.

During Jim's lost years, Irene would go on to claim power of attorney over his business affairs to halt his headlong dive into bankruptcy. At the same time, she managed to cram in three long and hard years of study and practical work to qualify as a State Registered Nurse.

Reluctantly, and for all the right reasons, she also began divorce proceedings. This most courageous and brave case of tough love would eventually prove to be the major factor in Jimmy's return from the wilderness.

Add to this the small matter of raising a family virtually single-handed, and it is no wonder, that anyone meeting Irene for the first time, will immediately realise they are in the presence of one remarkable lady.

It also proves that as long as there is true love, a happy ending is possible.

In 1977, in an attempt to beat his drink problem and add some structure to his life, Jim once again laced-up his boots and returned to football – this time with Barnet – then of the Southern League. Aware of his troubles and in a bid to save his good friend, Barnet Chairman Dave Underwood gently coaxed Jimmy back into the game.

Playing as a strolling midfield general in the Rivelino mould, Jim repaid Dave and Barnet with two seasons of outstanding service. He scored 16 goals in 55 games for 'The Bees' and was named the club's Player of the Year in 1978. He loved his footballing life at Underhill, but unfortunately the demon drink was still the main focus of his existence, and a brief spell with Woodford Town did not cure the thirst.

By the winter of 1978, Jimmy's life was out of control and Fleet Street had finally ferreted out the fact that he was having problems.

With his story about to hit the front pages and divorce imminent, Jim began his fight-back. He had been an undisciplined member of Alcoholics Anonymous for two years but now decided to have a real go at following their code of living.

On February 28th 1978, Jim finally took command of the biggest battle of his life and had his last drink. He and his journalist pal Norman Giller, then collaborating with him on his best-selling book *This One's On M*e, mutually agreed not to touch another drop. They toasted each other with sparkling water, saying: "Let's go and get sober out of our minds."

When speaking to him today, he never says last ever drink. Jimmy still considers himself an alcoholic. Once an alcoholic, always an alcoholic. But, as the AA doctrine states: today he is sober.

Jimmy and Noman were stopped in their tracks when their great mate Vic Railton, chief football writer for the London *Evening News* and one of their favourite characters, suddenly dropped down dead of a heart attack. He was 58. They went to Vic's funeral together and agreed that their stop-drinking pledge was vital. Jimmy knew that otherwise he would be joining Vic in the graveyard.

Jimmy on his last drink

‘I can be specific about the date and even the place where I had my last drop. It was eight days after my 38th birthday and I had been on an almighty bender that ended with me being taken into a ward for the mentally disturbed at Warley Hospital in Essex.

Fleet Street were on to the story, and on the Saturday evening before my shame was to be spread across the Sunday front pages I walked out of Warley Hospital and called in at the White Horse in Brentwood, which was the nearest pub. It was after 10 o'clock in the evening and the place was packed. I had to almost battle my way to the bar where I ordered a pint of best bitter and knocked it back without it touching the sides of my throat. It was a wonder I had any room for the liquid because over the previous fortnight I had drunk myself into a stupor. Yet I still had a raging thirst and, with just minutes to closing time, I ordered a second pint and that went down just as quickly.

The barman called 'Last Orders' and I started to push my way back towards the bar. I was jostled this way and that, and suddenly I said, 'Oh bollocks to it.' With that I walked out of the pub and away from boozing. I knew that from the moment the newspapers hit the doormats the next morning I would be on show, and I was determined to prove that I could beat it. Not since then has a drop of alcohol passed my lips.’

As news of his troubles became public, friends and well-wishers rallied to offer help and support. The two Normans – photographer Quicke and writer Giller – and their lovely wives, Jean and Eileen, were among the first to come to Jim's aid. Jimmy replaced booze with coffee, and started drinking lashings of it. While working with Norman Giller on an idea to become the Dick Francis of football thriller writers, he had his own coffee pot at the Giller household in Thorpe Bay, Essex.

It was there that he shot most of a television programme called *Just for Today*, directed by Bernie Stringle and based on Jimmy's *This One's On Me* book. Stringle, a Spurs season ticket holder and father of one of the world's top jazz clarinettists (Julian Marc Stringle), had Jimmy talking to camera for hours on end, little knowing that he was helping to forge a new career for our hero.

Jimmy finds a friend who has his cake and eats it ... but no drink to wash it down

Bernie was the genius behind the PG Chimp adverts, and Jimmy continually had the film crew in fits of laughter with jokes comparing himself with the chimps. The experience Jimmy was getting in front of the camera, talking off the cuff and without a note or an autocue, was to prove priceless. "This is so easy, a monkey could do it," said Jim to Bernie. "No wonder you are only paying me peanuts."

Within three months of their divorce becoming absolute, a sober and sane Jim moved back in with his beloved Irene and set about rebuilding his life.

Jimmy on his divorce

'Irene's decision to divorce me was just the jolt that I needed. Suddenly I had a target in life – to win back the woman I loved. I wanted her back more than anything in the world, and the only chance I had of doing that was if I stopped drinking. It was the greatest motivation I could possibly have had. Irene made it clear that if I wanted to come back permanantly into her life I was welcome provided I was never ever under the influence. I have been back with my Irene and with my fantastic kids ever since.'

Jimmy's first steps on the road to rehabilitation began in earnest with him courageously tackling his inner demons head-on in an honest and frank autobiography and an emotional, nerve-wracking TV appearance.

With endless cups of coffee replacing the booze and veiled in a heavy fog of cigarette smoke, Jimmy underwent long and gruelling interview sessions with only Norman Giller and a tape-recorder for company. *This One's On Me* – a raw and powerful purging of the soul that is a fascinating, unsettling account of Jim's downfall. To this day, alcoholics and people fearing a drink problem seek out the book for the no-punches-pulled advice that Jimmy offers within its pages.

In the spring of 1979, Jimmy travelled to the LWT studios to record an interview on the Russell Harty Plus show. As he waited in the wings and without the crutch of alcohol to settle his nerves, Jim seriously considered making an escape to the nearest bar. But, showing amazing resolve, he managed to make it on to the set and was quickly put at ease by Harty, a larger-than-life character who had a unique way of putting his questions (once famously getting slapped around the face by singer Grace Jones during a live chat). The greatest interviewers manage to delve deeply into the inner psyche of their subject while making it seem like an informal chat. The late Russell Harty was such a man. What followed was an extraordinarily candid interview in which an emotionally naked Jim poured his heart out.

Appreciating his courage and honesty, the public reaction to Jimmy's appearance was overwhelmingly positive. It really did seem that the whole of the nation had rallied to his side. Jimmy had majestically cleared the first hurdles in the long race to recovery.

Jimmy on the Russell Harty interview

❛I was visibly shaking with tension as I waited to make my entrance on to the set in front of a studio audience of a couple of hundred people. It was like a return to the boozer's shakes I had got to know so well. I was still having to fight the urge to turn and run away as I watched on a monitor while Russell read my introduction from an autocue.

Suddenly a floor manager was signalling me forward on to the set, and Russell Harty was announcing me as if I was somebody special. My confidence was so low that I felt anything but special. I just wanted to get the hell out of there.

I felt immediately at ease in Russell's company and, after a preamble about my footballing life, we got down to the nitty gritty. It was the moment I had been dreading since agreeing to do the interview. It was one thing admitting at a meeting of Alcoholics Anonymous that I was an alcoholic, and confessing it to a ghostwriter to be put down in black-and-white in a book. But to openly declare to millions of television viewers that I was an alcoholic was going to be, so I thought, one of the hardest things I had ever done in my life. But Russell had got me so relaxed with what was clearly a genuine interest in my problem that I found myself talking quite easily about the horrors of my drinking habit.

I felt like a released prisoner when the interview finally finished and could not wait to get back to the hospitality room for a drink. I felt everybody's eyes boring into me as I went to the bar and placed my order – for a large, iced – shaken not stirred – glass of Perrier water.

I will always remember Russell Harty with gratitude as one of the people who helped me make my comeback. It was very sad when he became an early victim of AIDS. **'**

At the time of the Harty interview, Jimmy was living in a tiny one-bedroom rented flat on the outskirts of London and making a Del-Boy-like living selling ladies' sweaters. The job was provided by knitwear fashion supplier Geoffrey Green, who generously went out of his way to help Jim through the hard times. The one luxury in Jimmy's debt-ridden existence at that time was not a yellow Reliant Robin, a la Trotter, but a yellow Jaguar XJ6 – priorities, Jim? He has always liked a nice motor, and nothing has changed.

In those early days of sobriety, Jimmy's contact with Irene and the children was restricted to weekend visits as he attempted to rebuild the broken bridges of trust with his family.

Having helped in the planning of the wedding of his eldest daughter, Lynn, Jimmy gradually succeeded in winning back Irene's confidence and, three months after their divorce had become absolute, Jim moved home.

The next phase in the Greaves rejuvenation was the quest for a post-football career and income. Norman Giller approached *The Sun's* legendary sports editor Frank Nicklin, and offered a weekly column. With the era of the ex-player-becoming-pundit just dawning, Nicklin just happened to be on the lookout for an opinionated legend with clout to fulfil the role for *The Sun*. Jim was the perfect man for the job. Just as in his playing career, he still had the incredible knack of being in the right place at the right time. It was the start of a 30-year link with what he calls 'the Currant Bun.' (He has since transferred to *The People,* with something less than a £99,999 fee involved).

The family that welcomed sober Jimmy back – celebrating here in 2009 the 50th wedding anniversary of Jim and Irene (centre): left, Andy with Lynn, and right, Mitzi with Danny. Truly a golden day for our hero.

Jim's forthright, no-nonsense views on the game made an immediate impact with *The Sun's* man-in-the-street reader and his columns soon became essential reading for millions of football fans.

Initially unsure of the long-term prospects of his role as a soccer pundit, Jim also secured a job with the Abbey Life Assurance Company. Under the guidance of his good friend Paul Revere, he quickly settled into the world of insurance and in no time was making presentations at major conferences as an Associate at Abbey Life. It was to prove a marvellous foundation for the launching of his own insurance brokerage company that he would later run with Lynn. Jim was not your cliché thick-as-two-planks, brains-in-the-feet stereotype footballer. He was highly intelligent, and now highly motivated. He had restored his dignity. Now he had a living to make, and the eyes of the world were on him to see if he would fall off the wagon. There were those witnesses of the last few years of his life who would have had no doubt that he would be back on the bottle. In hindsight, I can say they should not hold their breath!

Less than two years after hitting absolute rock bottom, Jimmy was now progressing at pace in his climb back up to life's summit. Gainfully employed and back in the bosom of his loving family, his life was about to take yet another unexpected and astonishing turn.

14: Sofa So Good on Television

IN August 1980, Jimmy was jogging along happily with his new life unaware that plans were being made to hunt him down and offer him the opportunity to return to the public limelight.

Tony Flanagan – producer of ATV's (now ITV Central) *Star Soccer* – was casting around for a former footballer to work as an analyst on his Saturday night show that featured action highlights of matches involving teams based in the Midlands. The names of a procession of ex-players with Midlands connections were considered and discarded, and then, Flanagan staggered his colleagues at an editorial meeting by saying, 'How about Greavsie?'

'Greavsie? But he's a pisshead.'

Tony tossed a copy of The Sun on to the desk. 'Well he's sober enough to produce an excellent column like this,' he said. 'He's obviously not frightened to speak his mind, and in that documentary, Just for Today he proved he could work to camera like a real pro.'

There were mumblings about it being a bit stupid having a Cockney commenting on the Midlands football scene, but Jimmy Hill, Malcolm Allison and John Bond had made the London accent acceptable to all ears. And so the call went out, 'Get Greavsie.'

Gary Newbon, *Star Soccer* editor and later the Head of Sport, contacted Norman Giller, who was not only ghosting Jimmy but also representing him. Norman then negotiated with Jimmy's old England skipper Billy Wright. It completed a circle, because Norman ghosted Billy Wright's column in the *Daily Express* when he was Arsenal manager before becoming an ATV executive

At first, a jittery Jim was reluctant to take up the offer. It took Irene to persuade him that it was a fabulous opportunity and to accept the job.

The first person Jim was introduced to by Gary Newbon on arriving at the ATV studios was the football reporter who would be working with them on the show. He was a young, fresh-faced journalist called Nick Owen. In the nearby newsroom a presenter was preparing her script ready for the local news round-up. She was Anne Diamond. Jim had no idea that the three of them were destined one day in the future to come together with an as yet unborn television company and in circumstances of high drama and, often, high farce – more of that later.

Next on the tour of his new stamping ground Jim was reunited with executive sports chief Billy Wright. At the end of his distinguished playing career Billy had wrestled unhappily with management at Arsenal before going into television management.

Somebody unkindly reminded Billy about the time Jimmy banged in the five goals against him in his final season with Wolves, when he was a seventeen-year-old whippersnapper with Chelsea and Billy was thirty-four

Billy then told this story against himself, 'I played hundreds of matches during my career, captained England and won 105 caps, skippered three championship-winning sides and lifted the FA Cup. But the only three things I seem to be remembered for are skippering the side beaten by the United States at the 1950 World Cup, being beaten all ends up when Puskas scored his wonder goal in Hungary's 6-3 win at Wembley, and continually tackling Jimmy's shadow when he scored those five goals against Wolves.'

'It's a funny old game, Bill,' Jim replied – a catchphrase was born.

Billy showed a few years later that he had not lost the iron will that made him such a great footballer and magnificent ambassador for the game and our country. He managed very quietly to beat the sort of booze problem that would have cut down lesser men. Just as with Jim, it was his greatest victory.

Jimmy's early performances on *Star Soccer* were shaky to say the least. A combination of nerves and a hatred of the autocue – his dyslexia again surfacing – saw Jim struggling to settle.

With Newbon and Owen always on hand to offer help and advice, Jim was encouraged to forget about scripts and tactical analysis and just be himself.

In his third appearance, by which time he had started to conquer his nerves, he was relaxed enough to talk about the game exactly as he would if he were standing on the terraces. There was an obvious offside goal that was allowed to stand, and Jim said: 'Blimey, if I'd scored that one I would have kissed the ref. And if I'd been in the opposition team I would have told the linesman where to stick his flag.'

It was the real Jim at his humorous best, and resulted in Gary Newbon laughing out loud and the technicians on the studio floor failing to contain their fits of laughter. From that moment on, Jimmy's television career was up and running.

The early press reviews of Jim's TV performances were as positive as those he received as a master marksman.

'Jimmy Greaves has brought something almost unheard of to football punditry – a sense of humour,' said the *Sunday Times*. 'Greavsie is the cheeky chappie of TV sport who has brought a rare and much-needed smile to the sad face of soccer,' said *The Sun*. 'He is irreverent, savagely honest, often hilarious and sometimes bordering on the irresponsible, which make his act compulsive viewing and certainly more entertaining

Many Thanks
+
Best Wishes
Jimmy Greaves

The autographed photo that Jimmy was sending to his fans in his Central TV days

than the football that he is analysing,' said the *Mail*.

Jimmy was thoroughly enjoying himself and had quickly settled into a routine at what was to become Central Television. His first season with the *Star Soccer* team went so well that he was given a larger canvas, and started to contribute a regular feature called The Greaves Report, in which he took an off-beat look at sport. Over the following months Jim played tennis with John McEnroe, faced Bob Willis bowling flat out, wrestled with Kendo Nagasaki, motor cycled with Barry Sheene, ran with Sebastian Coe, stepped-up to the oche with Eric Bristow and took on Jonah Barrington on the squash court.

As well as trying his hand at bowls, croquet, arm wrestling and fishing, he also gave the first out-of-the-ring television exposure to an up-and-coming young heavyweight called Frank Bruno.

His most terrifying experience on The Greaves Report came when Jim – a famously reluctant flyer – was somehow persuaded to take to the air in a two-man hang glider with professional pilot Rory McCarthy.

It was early December and a strong icy wind was blowing as they took off from Dunstable Downs in Bedfordshire. They were airborne for 10 minutes soaring at 300 feet above the Downs when the glider was caught by a sudden 60 mph gust. It swept them up towards the 1,000 feet mark, and McCarthy deliberately stalled the glider to stop them being blown towards a built-up area. Earthbound they plummeted, with Rory working like Superman to control their descent.

Eventually and with extreme good fortune, they landed in light bracken that broke their fall, and were lucky enough to land on top of the smashed glider. Both Rory and Jim were shaken and bruised, but escaped without injury.

Producer Jeff Farmer checked that they were all right, and then said: 'You were never any good in the air, Greavsie.'

Jim's first breakthrough on to network television came during the 1982 World Cup finals, when he was invited to be a member of the ITV panel under the chairmanship of the late, great voice of football, Brian Moore.

The line-up of panellists read like a who's who of outspoken football rebels of the era including George Best, Jack Charlton, Denis Law, Mike Channon, Ian St John and Brian Clough.

Moore, the master, somehow managed to maintain some kind of control throughout the competition as Jim and his cohorts attempted to turn the World Cup into a foot-and-mouth tournament.

By the end of the finals, Jimmy had emerged as the undoubted star of the show – starting and ending the tournament in peak form. On the first day of the finals, Jimmy was the only pundit to correctly pick eventual champions Italy as his favoured team to head home with the trophy. He did not sit on the fence. "Italy will be the champions," he said firmly, while most other pundits were picking two and three possible winners.

At the end of the final programme, after Italian captain Dino Zoff had lifted the World Cup, Brian Moore dangerously left the last word to Jimmy: 'These finals have all been about balls. Long balls, short balls, square balls, through balls, high balls, low balls, and to you, Brian, I would just like to say…(a deliberate pause)…it's been a pleasure being here on the panel.' With Brian on the verge of a nervous breakdown the end credits ran – classic Jimmy.

Unsurprisingly, Jim's stock shot up after his World Cup appearances and he received widespread praise in both the written and spoken media, and the public loved his cheeky asides. Almost immediately, the demand for interviews and personal appearances quadrupled. He had also made his mark with the chiefs of ITV and was rewarded with a regular spot on World of Sport, linking up 'live' with Ian St John in On the Ball from his base in Birmingham. This laid the foundation for what was to become the Saint and Greavsie show. And while all this was going on, the forces of fate were working to bring Anne Diamond, Nick Owen and Jimmy together in the unlikely setting of Camden Lock. They were all about to have indigestion for breakfast…

TV-am was launched in a blaze of publicity on February 1st 1983 spearheaded by the 'Famous Five' of David Frost, Michael Parkinson, Angela Rippon, Anna Ford and Robert Kee. The five legends were to present the ITV breakfast flagship and were also shareholders.

Before the first programme reached our TV screens, the ship was already sinking fast. When the individual contracts were sent out to the 'Famous Five' they were put into the wrong envelopes. You can imagine the explosive reactions when, purely by chance, Robert Kee found he was being paid less than Anna Ford, and Angela Rippon apparently discovered that her pay was paltry compared to the others. So before they even reached the airways there was dissent in the camp.

Just two months after their TV-am debuts, a resentful Angela Rippon and bitter Anna Ford walked away from the show. The dynamic Greg Dyke was brought in as Editor-in-Chief to try and save the station from the knackers yard. Norman Giller contacted Dyke and told him that Jimmy Greaves was the ideal man to present a hard-hitting sports opinion column of the air.

And so it was that in May 1983, Jimmy travelled with Norman to the 'state-of-the-art' TV-am studios – nicknamed 'Eggcup Towers' – to hold talks with Mr Dyke. Soon after their arrival, a London Electricity Board representative showed-up and gave the ultimatum that if the electricity bill was not paid within half-an-hour he would cut off the supply to the studios. One of the more surreal adventures in Jim's life had begun. Nothing in his football career had prepared him for this.

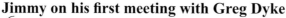

Jimmy on his first meeting with Greg Dyke

'What do you know about television?' was Greg Dyke's opening shot when I went into his office ready to pitch for the sports job.

'Enough to know which camera to look at when the red light comes on,' I said.

'No, not the camera side of television,' said Greg, 'I mean the important side that punters watch. Do you watch the box?'

'I've become a screenoholic since giving up the booze,' I said truthfully. 'I watch it until the little dot disappears after the epilogue.'

'Just what I wanted to hear,' said Greg, his eyes bulging with enthusiasm. 'You can be out television previewer. It will be a five-minute spot and I want you to tell viewers what they should and shouldn't watch. All I ask is that you do it with a bit of humour. No over-the-head highbrow stuff. We're looking to go down market.'

'That's very flattering of you,' I chuckled. 'You can't get much more down market than me.'

'No offence, Jim,' said Greg, who had so much energy pouring out of him that they could have plugged him into the mains and not had to worry about an electricity bill. 'I want us to become *The Sun* of the air, not the toffee-nosed *Telegraph* like the other lot made it.'

At this point Michael Parkinson, one of the survivors of 'the other lot,' and a *Telegraph* columnist, walked into the office. He and his wife Mary were holding the fort on air before going off to Australia for a summer break. 'Jimmy's joining us,' said Greg.

'Marvellous,' said Parky. 'Our sports coverage could do with some beefing up.'

'He's going to be our television previewer,' said Greg.

'Oh, I see,' said Parky, his eyes clouding over. 'That's, uh, very interesting.' Greavsie becoming the television previewer must have made as much sense to him as Bobby Charlton reading the news. As one of the founders of TV-am he had been under enormous pressure in the previous few weeks and looked shell-shocked and in need of that trip Down Under.'

Jimmy was among the first signings for the revamped breakfast show along with keep-fit expert 'Mad' Lizzie Webb and weather wise Wincey Willis. His old Birmingham side-kick Nick Owen, who had joined the original TV-am team as a sports presenter, was about to be promoted to full-time couch duty while Michael Parkinson was in Australia, with Henry Kelly joining as co-presenter. The enthusiastic Mike Morris would step into Nick's sports shoes, with a young sports reporter called Richard Keys coming in as his deputy. Dyke's next two signings fit the phrase 'from the sublime to the ridiculous perfectly' – Anne Diamond and Roland Rat. Thanks largely to Greg Dyke's policy of concentrating on 'popular' television, TV-am started to close the gap on BBC's Breakfast Time and in less than a year they had overhauled them in the ratings. But Jimmy and the team's self-congratulations were rather muted because everybody was giving the credit to Roland Rat for increasing their share of the audience. One rival across at the Beeb said, 'It's the first time a rat has come to the aid of a sinking ship.' Eventually Anne Diamond and Nick Owen finished up on the BBC sofa, and Roland the Rat also jumped ship and swam to the Beeb.

Jimmy's job on the sofa was made much easier by the back-up work of respected showbusiness journalist Joe Steeples, who did all the research for him and selected the clips of programmes that he was previewing. In January 1984 the TV-am news output was given a boost by the arrival of that master of newsreaders, Gordon Honeycombe.

As well as Good Morning Britain was doing in the ratings war with BBC's Breakfast Time, TV-am was losing money in a spectacular and worrying way. It was pouring away like blood out of a gaping wound. Jimmy had to wait weeks, sometimes months, for his fees and full-time staff members had to agree to take 'voluntary' pay cuts. Losses had spiralled to £12 million a year, and Camden Lock was running deep with rumours that the station was only weeks, perhaps days, from being closed down.

Bruce Gyngell, an eccentric, energetic Aussie, waltzed like a firebreathing Matilda into Eggcup Towers as managing director, and took on the unions, leading to a strike which almost brought the crisis station to its knees.

In 1990, changes in the law meant that ITV franchises were no longer allocated on merit or potential but rather through a blind auction. TV-am was outbid by another consortium, Sunrise Television – known as GMTV by its launch – and the slow, inexorable wind-up began. Over the next 18 months, TV-am as we knew it began to disappear piece-by-piece. The news service was axed and cartoons replaced Timmy Mallett's Wacaday.

Jim remained until the bitter end, taking his place on the sofa as the final show was broadcast on December 31st 1992. After nine eventful and crazy years, his breakfast television adventure was at an end.

Fortunately, all was not lost on the television front for Jimmy as he was already establishing himself as the funny man in a comedy double-act that was to raise his TV profile to its peak. Enter Saint and Greavsie…

15: *Saint and Greavsie*

IT was John Bromley – a close pal of Jimmy's and an executive at LWT – who came up with the idea for the Saint and Greavsie show. The Greaves and 'Brommers' friendship went back as far as the 'fifties, when Jim was just starting out on his professional footballing career with Chelsea and Bromley was a young local newspaper reporter in Essex. Brommers went on to become a respected sports journalist on the *Daily Herald* and then the *Daily Mirror* before moving into television.

Ian St John had already proved his ability at the microphone when he reached the final of a BBC competition to find a commentator, and he quickly confirmed that he was a television 'natural' when taking over from Brian Moore as presenter of On the Ball, which was the football slot on World of Sport.

Jimmy on his early impressions of The Saint

'I had tremendous respect for Ian as a player with Liverpool and Scotland, but in those days I never really knew him as a person. He always seemed surrounded by showbiz types. Jimmy Tarbuck remains one of his closest pals – and I got the impression he was a bit of a flash git.

He came back into my life after suffering some hard times trying to establish himself as a manager and coach. Saint's coaching ability was highly thought of in the game, particularly at Coventry and Sheffield Wednesday (where he was big Jack Charlton's right-hand man). He put his head on the block as manager at Portsmouth, and still carries the scars of an unhappy ending to his managerial career when he was sacked without having really been given a proper chance to show what he could do. Football's loss was television's gain."

The seeds for Saint and Greavsie were sown when Jim was invited to take part in a regular Saturday afternoon cross-talk with St John. Jim was at his Birmingham studio-base while Saint was in London. Their long-distance chat became so popular that John Bromley proposed a full-blown Saint and Greavsie show in the LWT studios after World of Sport had drawn its final breath in September 1985 after 20 years of in and out, up and down service.

At 12.05pm on October 5 1985, the first Saint and Greavsie show was broadcast on ITV. The natural chemistry between the two footballing greats, sharing a studio for the first time, raised their bantering to a whole new level of hilarity. It was the beginning of a seven-year, on-screen double-act that would provide unmissable entertainment to perfectly accompany the nation's lunch on a Saturday afternoon.

Jimmy on Saint and Greavsie

'At first, I didn't fancy doing the show one bit. Up to that point in my TV career I'd always been a support player and was more-than-happy in the role. The thought of taking on a 'starring' role frankly terrified me, but I was talked into it by Gary Newbon who convinced me it would be a good thing for my career. I think Gary now wishes he had kept his mouth shut, and then I might have remained a small time pundit and not got too big for my boots!

The way we worked on the show was exactly how I used to play football. I left The Saint to do all the hard graft – reading the autocue and setting up all the inserts – while I just concentrated on slipping in-and-out of the action with hopefully funny one-liners and comments on the main items.

The Saint and I were very lucky in having imaginative editors at the helm in Bob Patience and then Richard Worth, and we had excellent input to the show from ITV team members of the time – notably Martin Tyler, Alan Parry and Jim Rosenthal (now all true legends of the sport-talk game).

We set out to entertain and explain, in that order. We didn't think the vast majority of our viewers wanted us blinding them with science about what is only a game. If we did have to get deadly serious about things, the Saint and I had 78 caps between us to prove that we knew what we were talking about. Our bright and breezy approach meant we had to take a lot of stick from some 'serious' sections of the media who thought that we treated football too lightly. 'Saint and Greavsie are a couple of jokers who have managed to take football down to the level of a second-rate music hall act,' wrote one 'quality paper' scribe. Each to their own.'

During the early years of Saint and Greavsie, Jim frequently trod a tightrope on the programme when one trip of the tongue could have caused a lot of damage (or damages). Because it was live, the ITV lawyers watched with legal-eagle eyes in case

Saint and Greavsie with the 1990 World Cup mascot

he dropped himself, and them, into the mire. On one occasion, Jimmy was in it up to his neck following a match in which he said that the referee had sent-off a player just to get himself into history before he retires. The referee hit Jim with a writ for slander, and he was forced to apologise for his 'unwise' remark in the High Court and had to pick up the bill for the legal costs and also make a payment to the Referees' Association Benevolent Fund.

From that moment on Jimmy tried and, mostly succeeded, in becoming more guarded with his comments, making sure that he added 'in my opinion' when passing judgments. He had quickly discovered that you are entering a legal minefield when you start making an opinion sound like a statement of fact.

The show was a great adventure ride for both Ian and Jimmy. The Saint found himself being invited to play in top pro-am golf tournaments – I am sure if he ever gets to live his life over again he will come back as a golf professional. He is fanatical about the game. Jimmy got some great off-beat assignments, including golfing with Seve Ballesteros, boxing with Mike Tyson and clowning with the likes of Ian Botham, Frankie Dettori and his old mate Cloughie.

Jimmy also had input to other programmes, notably Sport In Question that was masterminded by former Saint and Greavsie producer Bob Patience, and ITV's answer to A Question of Sport – Sporting Triangles. Jimmy was captain of one team up against rivals led by former Liverpool and England captain Emlyn Hughes, who had been poached from BBC.

It is rare for Jimmy not to get on with people, but he and Emlyn took an early dislike to each other. They fell out to the point where Jimmy was prepared to walk away from the show and a lucrative contract. At the root of their problem was the fact that Hughes had a commercial contract to wear an exclusive sweater. That didn't bother Jim, but what did upset him was that he was ordered to wear the same style sweater, with the manufacturer's logo clearly showing. Jimmy dug in his heels and refused to wear the sweater, which led to him falling out with his old Central TV chums Gary Newbon and Jeff Farmer. Peace was finally restored but the damage had been done, and the atmosphere in the small, talented Central team was never quite as friendly and laid-back. Jimmy hated upsetting his old friends but it was a matter of principle. He was greatly upset when Emlyn died early, and the subject of the sweaters is now taboo.

The Saint and Greavsie Show won several awards as the best sports programme on television, but as so often happens in life when things are travelling along swimmingly, a bombshell is likely to fall and explode to throw everything into chaos and confusion. In the summer of 1992, such a metaphoric device detonated on Jimmy's world – and onto the whole universe of professional football and television in the UK.

With Jimmy and St John still in peak form after seven happy years on ITV, a deal was struck that was to revolutionise English football – like never before or since – whilst bringing Jimmy's TV career to an abrupt halt. The newly formed Premier League agreed an exclusive contract with the interloping satellite powerhouse that was Sky TV and, in the blink of an eye, terrestrial channels had lost all live televisual football rights. The life of the armchair sports fan would never be the same again.

Within a fortnight of the agreement, Saint and Greavsie was unceremoniously axed from the ITV schedules. The final shows were broadcast from Sweden during the 1992 European championships. In the very last programme and, after making a series of stinging jokes at Sky's expense, the Saint and Greavsie show drew to a close with Jimmy and Ian singing 'This could be the last time' as the end credits rolled.

Another chapter in Jimmy's incredible life had reached its conclusion.

Ever since the final curtain fell on Saint and Greavsie, television producers have tried and, in the minds of most, miserably failed to replicate the easy-going, light-hearted yet authoritative take on football that Jim and Ian made look oh-so simple.

From the alleged 'cutting-edge satire' of Skinner and Baddiel through to the entertaining but limited appeal of Sky's laddish Soccer Am, the special ingredients have been missing – knowledge, charisma and likeability.

At Wembley Stadium on May 30th 2009, the morning of the FA Cup final between Chelsea and Everton, a regretfully small audience was reminded of what we had all been missing when Jim and The Saint made a memorable comeback to the small screen on the short-lived satellite channel Setanta Sports for a one-off Cup final preview. It proved to be a triumphant return – reminiscent of a parade of homecoming heroes. Setanta closed down shortly after. "Hope they don't blame us," said Jim.

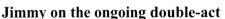

Jimmy on the ongoing double-act

'I got most of the punchlines on the Saint and Greavsie show, but the Saint is a very funny man in his own right. Over the years, since the demise of the Saint and Greavsie show, we have made many personal appearances together and Ian always goes down well with a sense of humour that can be as cutting as a claymore. In fact, on a golf course he has been known to slice a ball in two with his language! Since getting to really know Saint, we have always got on well – off as well as on stage and screen. But we only see each other when we're working. We're not into each other's pockets (you would need a jemmy to get into the Saint's pocket). Morecambe and Wise were my favourite double act. The Saint is the wise man of our partnership, even down to the wig – he'll kick me in the kilt for letting on about that one!'

With this book about to head for the presses, many campaigns are gathering momentum calling for a permanent restoration of the 'dynamic duo' to our television screens. As I write, the Facebook group 'Ban Soccer AM, Bring Back Saint and Greavsie' is recruiting countless members with each passing week. Who knows what the TV future holds for Saint and Greavsie?

Here's an exclusive quote from realist Jim: "Don't hold your breath."

The television viewers realised what they had been missing when Jimmy gave a half-time interview during the 2009 World Cup qualifier between England and Andorra. It was the day he received his World Cup medal. Asked about the match, he pretended not even to know England's opponents.

'Andorra?' Jim queried. 'Are they a village side? I've never seen such a bad team in my life. I mean that.'

The TV producers hurriedly moved him off camera. Nobody must be honest and knock the product.

'I was sitting in the stands with all the members of the 1966 squad,' Jimmy told me, 'and we were looking at each other, all of us thinking, "Why didn't we get to play teams like this?" We couldn't believe what we were watching. So I said what we all thought. When I worked in television you didn't have to wear rose-coloured glasses at the game. You watch a match now, at half-time a bloke comes on, flashes his teeth and tells you it's fabulous. And I'm thinking, "No, mate, it is crap".

'I watch rugby and think there are men out there, playing. I'm not so sure about football now. Players score and they've got to wipe their arse on the corner flag or dive on the ground as if they have found God. It is alien, all that nonsense. And what's that about, putting your finger to your lips? You've scored a goal. That's your job. Then they clutch their shirt badge, players who don't know the history of the club for which they are playing or what loyalty means. Get back to the halfway line and get on with it. Me, by then I've turned over to the rugby."

Let's leave Victor Meldrew behind (nodding our agreement) and get back to the James Peter Greaves story. Within the space of a year in the early 'nineties, his TV work had all but disappeared. Yet Jim was content. He was financially secure and living a happy existence with Irene as a proud and happy father and grandfather – but something was missing. At a time of life when most people would be considering a leisurely journey towards retirement, Jimmy still had ambition.

As fate would decree, a middle-aged Dorset-based former DJ would at the same time be embarking on a new career as an agent, representative and sports memorabilia distributor in search of the perfect client. His hero and intended target happened to be the still-hungry Jimmy Greaves and his name happened to be Terry Baker. My turn for the spotlight.

In his prime, Jimmy and Gordon Brown find a lot to laugh about at 10 Downing Street

IHAVE managed to keep a fairly low profile on my way through describing the life and times of my hero Jimmy Greaves, but now I need to come out in the open to share with you the incredible adventure that we are having together. Jimmy and I have been a sort of double act for longer than he was on television with the Saint; we are up to fifteen years and, hopefully, with several more to go before he wears me out.

At seventy, Jimmy has the energy and enthusiasm of somebody half his age. I have promoted him (and appeared with him) in more than 300 stage shows around the UK and never cease to wonder at his ability to entertain and enlighten audiences from across the generations. In every show, you can almost reach out and feel the warmth for the little (ok, and rotund) ex-footballer who does not quite realise that he is cherished as a national treasure.

There is not a conceited bone in Jimmy's body, so he has no idea that people from all walks of life, of both and indetermined sexes, young and old and every imaginable profession love him. Yes, Jim, I do mean *love*.

He gave me the privilege of accompanying him when he went to No 10 Downing Street in 2009 to – at long last – collect his medal for being a member of the triumphant 1966 World Cup squad. Perhaps this is a good moment to point out that I work regularly with the surviving members of the winning team of '66, also Frank Bruno and Ricky Hatton and, oh yes, in Europe, the one and only Pele, and also Ossie Ardiles and Ricky Villa among a few dozen others. I am putting flesh on my bones so that you know that Jimmy is in good hands, and I love him like a brother.

Anyway, back to Number 10: Prime Minister Gordon Brown, famous for looking grumpy and with a face like thunder, relaxed so much in Jimmy's company that I thought he was going to fall over laughing. This is the effect Jimmy has on people, and the PM showed him the sort of affection he wins from everybody – even the Scots, to whom, tongue in cheek, he gives huge stick.

Jimmy was fairly bruised and disillusioned when he came into my life. Along with my wife and business partner, Freda, we invited him to give an after-dinner speech in Bournemouth from where we run our A1 Sports Memorabilia business. He had recently been ditched by ITV – along with Ian St John – after they had made the *Saint and Greavsie* show the most popular sports programme on television.

He had also, thankfully, lost his *Greavsie's Gaff* show, that even Jimmy admits was car crash television at its worst (or perhaps that should be it's funniest). This had been produced by former *This Is Your Life* scriptwriter Roy Bottomley, who took over and changed a format that had worked really well for Jim in a Midlands-only chat show series. By the time the programme went national it was, well, a total mess. Roy seemed to think he was working with an experienced broadcaster like Eamonn Andrews, and stretched Our Jim to breaking point by asking him to do things that were just not in his compass. The result was – and this is our hero's description – Jim 'dying on his arse' in front of the camera as he tried to handle celebrity interviews while attempting to be himself. His good friend Joe Steeples, who had been such a strength to him at TV-am, tried to improve the script but got little encouragement from Bottomley, who – according to Jim – had a very high opinion of himself for such a short man.

At one stage during backroom bickering Jim had him pinned to the wall. I have painted Jim as a bit of a pussycat, but he can erupt like a volcano if he feels he is being misused. It reached the point where Jim became something of a laughing stock because of the cock-ups and unintended humour in the show. Skinner and Baddiel – nowhere near as entertaining as Jim – had a section of their chat show devoted to spotlighting Jim's gaffes. Jim had the balls to appear on their sofa and tell them to their face: "You're taking the piss." But it was hold-your-hands-up time, and Jimmy admitted that the show deserved its pounding criticism.

 **Jimmy on Greavsie's Gaff**

❛That was my unhappiest time in TV. We had a really good, laid-back, gentle weekly programme going at Central, produced and directed by the local team and everybody enjoying it, including the viewers. It was so successful that it was decided to put it out nationwide. If they had just left us to do our own thing, I am sure everything would have been fine. But Roy Bottomley, a vastly experienced programme maker, was brought in, and – to use one of his favourite sayings – 'we want celebrity gold dust and glamour.' Before I knew where I was I was interviewing Page 3 girls and second-rate stars interested only in plugging their latest book or video. I can't put all the blame on Roy. I became as stiff as a board in front of the camera because I was having to work to a tight script and deadlines, while any success I'd had was because I was allowed to be natural and do things off the cuff. *Saint and Greavsie* worked because Ian was a brilliant anchorman, while I was there just to chip in opinions and some jokes. It was the same as how I worked with Gary Newbon on Central sport. Bottomley was expecting me to be Eamonn Andrews and I was more like Julie. It could only end in tears.❜

The *Greavsie's Gaff* became known as *Greavsie's Gaffe* and it deserved to get the chop, but ITV made a huge miscalculation in axing *Saint and Greavsie*. It was their football flagship and it went down with all hands in 1992, and much of the vast five million Saturday lunchtime audience disappeared with them.

So the Jimmy Greaves I met in Bournemouth was, to say the least, pissed off with television and was looking for a new way to make – in Jimmy jargon – a nice little earner.

I had been a prominent south coast DJ, and so was used to having a microphone in my hand and talking my head off, and I suggested to Jim it might be a good idea for him to take part in a series of 'An Audience with ...' type shows, where I would introduce him and then he take questions from the people who had paid to see him.

Anybody who has been to one of our shows will, I am sure, confirm that it works to perfection. Jimmy took to it like a duck to water and so, in his mid-50s, he launched career number three. First there had been the footballer beyond compare, then the television star and now the stage performer.

A naturally funny man, he added to his ad-libbing a well worked out stand-up comedy routine. I have lost count of the number of people who have told me he is one of the best stand-ups in the country. It is an art he has learned late in life and – like everything he has done (including his drinking) – he has tried to be the best.

Jimmy's humour is not for the faint-hearted. His anglo-Saxon language is as cutting as a sword, but always used to get best effect for his jokes and anecdotes. When facing the question-and-answer section of his show he takes no prisoners, and tells tales out of school that make people gasp and giggle in equal measure. He is not only a fine comedian but also a born raconteur. Perhaps it's the Irish blood coming out, but he can talk a donkey into the ground. But he is never ever boring.

For a few months I promoted a Greavsie and Best tour – and I have the lost hair to show for it! George, as loveable a bloke as you could meet, used to join us on stage. The shows were unpredictable, and always ended with standing ovations for the two icons of football. Jimmy never used to try to stop George drinking. "It's his life," Jimmy said. "He told me that he has chosen his way, and that it was different to mine. He had decided to continue to drink, I had decided to stop. Who's to say which of us was right? George went the way he wanted to. Perhaps he got more fun out of life than I did. He certainly had a bigger adventure than anybody else I know."

I am proud and privileged to be a motivating force in this third phase of Jimmy's remarkable life. I know him better than almost anybody apart from his lovely Irene at this stage as he reaches his seventh decade, and I can report that Jimmy has mellowed into a likeable – loveable even – and, dare I say, cuddly avuncular character, with an opinion on all things and sometimes straying into Grumpy Old Man territory. He is by

Me, with my friend, my hero and my stage companion, James Peter Greaves

some distance the wittiest man ever to cross my path. He will hate me revealing this, but he can also be enormously but anonymously generous. Our mutual mate Norman Giller was diagnosed with the same sort of bowel cancer that beat their buddy Bobby Moore. Emergency surgery saved Norman and in return he helped organise a fund-raising dinner for the Wessex Cancer Trust. Jimmy was the celebrity guest and did a fantastic stand-up act. When it came time for the club secretary to pay Jim his fee, he waived it and presented it to the Fund. I am going to be in trouble for telling this story, but Norman has insisted. We both want people to know the *real* Jimmy Greaves.

We tend to forget the price our heroes pay for their gifts. Jimmy has had two what he calls new knees fitted, and has gone through the pain and discomfort without any moaning or groaning. Yet he can still get around the golf course in low figures, and makes light of what has been a painful descent into old age. Sorry Jim, middle age.

As a Spurs nut, I am always trying to get Jimmy to tell me about his days as the best finisher ever to pull on the Lilywhite shirt. But he is so modest I almost have to hit him to recall properly his golden goals, like the ones that lit up the '60s against Manchester United, Newcastle and Leicester City that remain bright in the memories of those lucky to have witnessed them. I have never once known Jimmy boast about what he achieved in football. I was a fan of his from the first time I saw him play on television, when he scored in the third minute against Burnley in the 1962 FA Cup final. I was then a boy of seven ... now my hero is a man of seventy.

The Jimmy Greaves who has reached his three score years and ten is proudest of all of the family he has produced, four wonderful grown-up children – Lynn, Danny, Mitzi and Andrew – and a tribe of twelve grandchildren and, so far, one great-grandchild. He and Irene are blissfully happy together, and he will always be grateful for the way she brought him back from those dark, lost days of the drinking phase of his life.

There is a bit of Victor Meldrew creeping into him, particularly if you get him on the subject of politics ("They're all as bad as each other"), or talking about today's footballers. He does not mind them pocketing vast amounts provided they earn it. He thinks there are two many foreign mercenaries – "taking the money and then not running." But all in all he is happy with his lot, and looks forward to contuining with our stage shows until, as he puts it, "the public sack me."

That's the end of my input to the Jimmy Greaves at 70 life story. I am now going to hand over to the old boy himself, and then friends of his for their memories of Our Hero before the most important people –the fans – get their say.

Thanks, Jim, for your friendship, for your entertainment, your company and for all the memorable moments you gave me – and millions of others – on the football field. I hope this book does your career and your life justice.

It was a pleasure being a spectator. You made it a GREAT old game.

AS I wanted – in the best Jimmy Greaves traditions – to leave you laughing, here is a collection of the funniest true stories that Jimmy has told me during our years together. I have picked them carefully to make sure I do not steal from his stage and after-dinner material, which – frankly – would need to be printed on asbestos rather than paper! So now it's over to Jimmy, proving it really is a funny old game, and we kick off with a couple of tales about our mutual old friend Alan Ball, who – like Bobby Moore – left us all too early ...

⁶Alan Ball was a good mate, and we used to swap a lot of stories. He told me of the day he was leaving Goodison in a hurry to join the England squad for a summer tour during his days as an idol at Everton. He was holding a suitcase in either hand, and was confronted by an Everton supporter.

"'Ere, Al pal, gi's yer autograph," he said in thick Scouse as he held a blank piece of paper under Ballie's nose.

"Can't you see I've got my hands full?" said Ballie, desperate to catch a train.

"Don't worry, Al pal," said the fan. "Just spit on the paper. That'll do me."

When Alf Ramsey first selected Norman 'Bites Yer Legs' Hunter in an England team to meet Spain in Madrid, Ballie called for hush in the dressing-room. He then put his hands together and said with bowed head: "For what they are about to receive ..."⁹

Jimmy on George Best ...

⁶George used to have me in fits with his stories. He once went through an entire game in which, to win a bet, he played the ball only with his left foot. In another match, he passed the ball only to team-mate David Sadler, who was playing in the middle of the Man United defence at the time. "David had moaned at me before the match that I never passed the ball to him," said George. "He was sick to death of receiving it by the time the game was over.

George did everything by the bucketload. He played football better than almost anybody on the planet, he loved many of the women he bedded (which was on the Casanova scale), he drank more than was good for him but loved

Alan Ball was the 'baby' of the 1966 World Cup winning team and so it came as a massive shock when he died in 2007 at the all too young age of 61. Greavsie and Ballie were good pals. "He was not only an exceptional footballer but a lovely bloke," says Jimmy. "We had some good times together, and he is greatly missed."

every drop, and he spent every penny as if money was coming out of a tap. It was George, of course, who famously said: "I've spent my money on booze, women and fast cars, the rest I squandered."

Everybody, the world and its brother, had an opinion on George. And d'you know something, he didn't give a monkey's about any of them. He lived his life the way he wanted to, and – surprisingly, for somebody pictured so many times with a tasty blonde on his arm – he was happiest as a loner. He once told me that his most contented times were sitting alone at Continental-type cafés just watching the world go by. For all his exposure across front pages and on the box, he remained a shy man at heart.

George cared about other people that other people didn't care about. I remember before one of our road shows up in Leeds we were sitting having a meal in a pizza restaurant when, shuffling in, came the vaguely familiar figure of somebody we suddenly realised had been a pioneering player when George was first making his name in the game.

It was Albert Johanneson, the black South African winger, who had been a runner-up in the 1965 FA Cup final with Leeds. He had gone on the skids after his retirement and had become yet another loser to booze.

I left George and Albert talking over old times to get prepared for the evening's show. Bestie, not for the first time, failed to turn up, and later admitted that he and Albert had gone out on the piss.

"Well,' said George, "I at least had the satisfaction of giving Albert one more decent night out. Nobody gives a f*** about him. He deserved my full attention for just one night."

That was all logical to George. There will never be another like him.

Jimmy on funny goals ...

One of the funniest goals I scored came in a derby match against Fulham at Craven Cottage. Their goalie was Tony Macedo, who was born in Gibraltar and while usually reliable could sometimes become a crumbling rock at the back of the Fulham defence.

Tony had been to see the Harlem Globetrotters giving a basketball exhibition a couple of days before our game. As he collected the ball early in the game, he started to give an impersonation of the Globetrotters. He ran round the penalty area bouncing the ball and crouched in the style of Meadowlark Lemon, the star dribbler of the Globetrotters

Inspired by the cheers of the crowd, Tony mimed Meadowlark-style as if to throw the ball to an opponent – me, standing unmarked on the edge of the penalty area. He switched his aim to Fulham skipper Johnny Haynes, but the ball slipped out of his hand and landed at my feet All I had to do was side-foot the ball into the empty net. I couldn't resist shouting to Tony: "You silly basket." What Johnny Haynes called him is unprintable!

One of the funniest goals ever has to be the one scored by Leeds goalkeeper Gary Sprake against Leeds in a top-of-the-table clash at Anfield in the 1960s. Sprake meant to throw the ball to a team-mate, but it slipped out of his hand and flew into the top corner of the net.

The Saint played in that game and he said that most of the Leeds players had their backs to the goal and did not know what had happened. Jack Chalrton said to referee Jim Finney, "What the f***'s going on?" Jim repled: "Your goalkeeper has just thrown the ball into his own net, and I am awarding a goal."

The Kop choir broke into choruses of *Careless Hands*, which was a Des O'Connorr hit song at the time.❞

Jimmy on the funniest goal he ever saw

❝It was early in my career with Chelsea and we were playing Everton in a League match when a long shot slipped under the body of our England international goalkeeper Reg Matthews. Reg scrambled up and chased after the ball, hotly challenged by our big, bold captain Peter Sillett who thought he had a better chance of clearing it. They pounded neck and neck towards our goal. Reg won the race and then, instead of diving on the ball, elected to kick it away. He pivoted beautifully and cracked the ball dead centre – straight into the pit of Peter's stomach. The ball rebounded into the back of the net and Peter collapsed holding his stomach. The rest of us players collapsed holding our stomachs laughing. It was one of the all-time unforgettable goals that belonged in a *Carry On* football script.

There was a hilarious own goal at Tottenham shortly after I left, and it involved one of the nicest blokes I ever met in the game ... Cyril Knowles. Tottenham were coasting to victory against Crystal Palace at the Lane when the often eccentric Cyril casually kicked the ball back over his head from forty yards, taking it for granted that Pat Jennings would collect it. Pat had not had a shot to save all afternoon and was on gardening duty at the front of the penalty box, replacing divots in the pitch. He scurried back to try to catch the ball but could only watch as it bounced into the empty net. Nice one, Cyril!❞

Jimmy with a shaggy dog story ...

❛One of the funniest yet at the same time foulest things that ever happened to me on a football pitch was during the 1962 World Cup finals in Chile. England were playing Brazil in the quarter-final when a stray dog invaded the pitch during the first-half. It led a posse of ball boys and players a dance before I went down on all fours to capture it. He seemed very relieved as I handed him to an official. So relieved, in fact, that he rewarded me by pissing all the way down the front of my England shirt and shorts.

In those days there were no second kits provided, so I could not change at half-time and ponged all through the game. Garrincha, an animal-loving country boy who kept, among other things, fifty birds in his village home, fell in love with the stray. He saw the dog as a lucky omen because of the unbelievable game he – Garrincha, not the dog! – had against us, and took it home to Brazil with him.

After their 3-1 victory, he told reporters that he was going to name the dog after me, 'Yimmy Greaves'. He was barking mad.❜

Jimmy goes to the dogs ...

❛Cockney comedian Tommy Trinder was one of football's outstanding personalities when he was chairman of Fulham. The funniest thing he ever said was, "I'll make Johnny Haynes the first £100-a-week footballer."

Fulham were a very relaxed club in those days, and Tommy once walked into the dressing-room at Craven Cottage to find trainer Frank Penn massaging a greyhound.

"What's that?" asked Tommy. "Our new centre-forward?"

'It's a greyhound," said the trainer.

"I can see that," said Tommy. "But what's it doing here?"

"It belongs to Charlie Mitten," explained Frank. "We're getting it into the mood for tonight's big race."

Charlie Mitten, Fulham's outside-left who could have been a prototype for Del-Boy Trotter, came in at this point.

"There you are, guv'nor," said Charlie. "Been looking for you to tell you about the dog."

Tommy, accustomed to Charlie's ducking and diving, replied: "Oh, that's most considerate of you to tell me that we've given a bloody greyhound the run of Craven Cottage."

"Do yourself a favour, guv'nor," said cheeky Charlie, "and get your pound notes on it. It's running at Slough tonight and it's a racing certainty to finish first."

"But you can't train greyhounds here," protested Tommy. "This is a football club. Well, that's what I'm led to believe."

"I think you'll have to turn a blind eye just this once, guv'nor," said Charlie, famous for his persuasive tongue. "All the players have got their money on it, and it'll upset them if we upset the dog."

Tommy knew when he was beaten. He shrugged and handed Charlie a white fiver. "Here," he said. "put this on for me when you go to the track."

The dog trailed in last.•

Jimmy on the Toothless Tiger Nobby Stiles

•My old England team-mate Nobby Stiles, who autographed my shins in our playing days, often had me offering up a prayer of thanks in England games that he was on my side and not against me. He was only a little bloke but could dig like a heavyweight.

Nobby was once was in trouble with referee Pat Partridge when Man United were playing Burnley in a floodlit match at Old Trafford. He kept snapping away at the heels of Burnley centre-forward Andy Lochhead, and was twice quietly warned 'watch it' by the ref.

Partridge, good enough to referee in the 1978 World Cup finals, finally lost his patience with Our Nobby, and got his book out in the second-half after Nobby's badly timed tackle had sent Lochhead tumbling.

"But it's the floodlights, ref!" Nobby protested. "They shine in my contact lenses and I can't see a bloody thing."

Mr Partridge was unimpressed and started to write Nobby's name in his book, mis-spelling it Styles.

Nobby peered over his shoulder and said: "You can't even get my bloody name right."

Partridge countered: "I'm surprised you can read with the floodlights shining on your contact lenses."

Nobby gave a toothless grin. "Nice one, ref," he said. "Spell it how you like."

I liked the tongue in cheek quote from Sir Matt Busby when questioned about Nobby's ferocious tackling. He said: "Nobby a dirty player? No, he's never deliberately hurt anybody. Mind you, he's frightened quite a few."•

Saint and Greavsie feel the power of Frank Bruno ... getting Jim in the mood for an even tougher opponent, Iron Mike Tyson!

Jimmy, mainly through his television work, has met just about anybody who is anybody in the sports world. He held me spellbound with this tale of when he got into the ring with the one and only Mike Tyson ...

•It was one of my most memorable television interviews for our Saint and Greavsie show. At the time Tyson was being billed as the 'Baddest Man on the Planet'. I met him in his training camp tucked away in the Catskill Mountains in New York, where he was preparing for his world title defence against Michael Spinks in Atlantic City.

He trained in a small gymnasium above the cop shop in what was a one-horse town. As I watched him belting sparring partners around the ring as if they were punch bags, I got the feeling that I would not want to tango with Tyson, let alone tangle with him. I honestly felt I was in the presence of a being from another planet. The first thing that struck me about him was his cliff wall-face of a body, and in particular a neck that looked as if it might once have been a smoke stack on a tug. But it was not just his physical appearance that was so impressive and also intimidating. He had an aura about him that was almost electric, or even nuclear.

Back in the mid-60s I had met Muhammad Ali when he was in London training for his second fight with Henry Cooper. He too had an aura, but it was one that brought a smile to your face. Tyson brought a chill to the heart. With Ali you felt you were in the company as much of a great entertainer as a great sportsman. With Tyson, the feeling was more of being close to an unexploded bomb. I got a close-up sense of his strength and power when I climbed into the ring to chat with him in front of the television cameras.

He gave me a riveting fifteen-minute interview during which he playfully patted me in the ribs, and left a small bruise that I wore like a badge of honour. Mike sounded like a surgeon about to perform a cutting operation as he showed me how he went about mounting a body attack. "The main target area," he said as he pushed me into a corner of the ring under a mock (thank God) assault "are the liver, the kidney region, the heart, the floating rib and the abdomen."

I naively said that I thought kidney punches were illegal, and he laughed like a drain. "Hey, man, we're not talking Marquess of Queensbury rules here," he said. "I'm defending the world heavyweight championship, the greatest prize in sport. If you can get on the referee's blind side and land a punch to the kidneys, that's all part and parcel of the fight game."

It was like being in the company of an animal. He brought his massive right fist up into my soft underbelly. "Then there's the solar plexus punch," he said. "It was invented by that great English fighter of yours, Bob Fitzsimmons, when he knocked out James J. Corbett to become the world heavyweight champion. It was a remarkable performance by Fitz because he weighed no more than a middleweight."

Tyson peppered his conversation on camera and off with boxing facts. He's a genuine fan of his sport, and a walking record book on its history. I've never spoken to anybody quite like him. He is an uneducated man from the dead end of Brooklyn, yet talked to me like somebody who has swallowed a dictionary. He wouldn't win any prizes in the academic world, but has street sense of Mastermind proportion.

Mike and I had a long off-camera chat as he was changing in the locker room. One thing I can reveal is that the most impressive part of his anatomy was never seen in public. I'll leave it to your imagination. Let's just say he could have swept the gymnasium floor without a broom! Yet he had a surprisingly high, almost effeminate voice and a slight lisp.

I asked him what it was like to land a knockout punch, and he replied: "Better than the greatest orgasm you could ever have."

He told me he'd never forgotten that he'd come from the streets. "I go back to my old neighbourhood a lot," he said. "It does me good to remind myself where my roots are. Man, they are the toughest streets on God's earth. Everybody has to fight just to survive. I go to prisons and drug rehabilitation centres just to give people hope. It makes you want to cry to see old friends who failed to beat the trap into which they were born."

He later, of course, got to know the inside of prison for real. He got put away for rape that pretty much destroyed his image and made commentators reach for the old saying that 'you can take the man out of the ghetto, but you can't take the ghetto out of the man.'

Mike, with the help of a lot of people, went through millions of dollars. I got just a taste of his lifestyle when three brand new Cadillacs were driven up to the gym, each a different colour. Mike came and sat behind the wheel of each one, and just couldn't make up his mind which one he liked best. So he ordered all three! That was just a hint that he was not going to hang on to his money for long.

While I was waiting for Mike to choose his car, one of his entourage, who worked the corner as the man in charge of the ice bucket, told me a true, funny story. During one fight they somehow forgot to take the icebag to the ring. This rarely mattered early in his career, because he battered his opponents into quick submission. The night they forgot the icebag Mike got a swelling under an eye. Panic! But the problem was solved when one of the quick-thinking cornermen took a condom out of his wallet, which he filled with iced water and then placed it under Tyson's eye. Somebody said – but not to his face– that it made him look a real dickhead.**'**

Jimmy still with the boxing gloves on ...

'I played in the match in which my Tottenham team-mate Terry Venables and Fulham defender Fred Callaghan famously got sent off for fighting at White Hart Lane. It was a few days after Muhammad Ali had defended his world title with a points victory over Ernie Terrell. During a viciously one-sided contest Ali – who had just recently changed his name from Cassius Clay – kept baiting the outclassed Terrell by saying: "What's mah name?"

"As Venners and Fred Callaghan – who had grown up together in the same Dagenham streets as me – stood sparring with each other, a voice from The Shelf pleaded: "For Gawd's sake, Tel, tell him yer name …!" The referee didn't see the joke, and sent them both off. It's a funny old game!

I used to go to the big fights with Bobby Moore, who was a keen fight fan. We were at Wembley the night Jerry Quarry, former world heavyweight title challenger, knocked out Jack Bodell, the chicken farmer from Swadlincote, in just 64 seconds. In the dressing-room after his demolition job, Quarry told reporters: "I knew nothing about Bodell apart from I'd been told he was big and awkward. This proved accurate information. He was very big and he fell very awkwardly.**'**

Jimmy with more boxing stories ...

'My old ITV colleague Reg Gutteridge once won fifty dollars off the then world heavyweight champion Sonny Liston. They were talking about pain thresholds, and Reg bet him that he could stick a knife in his leg without even blinking. Sonny, a born gambler, took the bet, and then watched as Reg stabbed his leg with a knife … without blinking. Reggie said that Sonny paid up and then fell over laughing when he rolled up his trouser leg to reveal he had a false leg. He had a leg blown off when he stepped on a mine during the Normandy D-Day landings.

One more boxing story that I heard at a sporsman's lunch, and it tickled me. See what you think. Pat Desmond, a fighter who had the gift of the gab as well as the gift of the jab, was taking a hammering in an all-Ireland heavyweight championship contest and went down on his knees in his own corner early in the second round. His second shouted, "Don't get up till nine, Pat … don't get up till nine …"

Still kneeling, Pat shouted back: "And what time is it now?"❜

Jimmy on Dickie Bird ...

❛I have got to know Dickie Bird well on the after-dinner speaking circuit, and he is eccentric but likeable with it. In the early days of mobile telephones he was standing in the middle umpiring a match at Northampton when Allan Lamb came in to bat. He handed Dickie one of the new-fangled phones and said, "Meant to leave this in the dressing-room. Look after it for me, Dickie." Those were the days when the mobile phone was the size of a brick. Five minutes later the telephone rang, and Dickie jumped a foot in the air. Lamby, at the other end, shouted: "Answer it Dickie, and tell them to ring back."

Dickie did as he was asked, and fumed when he found it was Ian Botham on the line asking him the score, and if he could speak to Lamby."

I think he might have made this bit up, but told me he said to Both: "Hang on. He won't be in for long."❜

Jimmy on David 'Biggles' Gower ...

❛When I first signed for Chelsea as a kid my dream was to be an all-rounder, playing football in the winter and cricket in the summer. I was a fair wicket-keeper, and idolised Godfrey Evans. But Chelsea manager Ted Drake told me the days of all-rounders were over, and talked me into giving all my concentration to football. It was a bit strong coming from Ted, who had played for Arsenal and played cricket for Hampshire.

Anyway, I have always followed cricket closely and loved Davd Gower's approach to to the game. He was the original 'Mr Cool.' David never gave the impression of thinking that cricket was a game of life or death. In one match batting for Leicestershire against Cambridge University, he decided to take runs only when he played the ball on the 'on' side. He kept the plan to himself, and his startled partner could not understand why he was continually sent back when the ball went from Gower's bat to the off side.

Gower later explained: "To be honest, I found myself getting very bored out there so I devised this little private game to keep myself alert. The few

I am presenting Jimmy with his 70th birthday cake at the O2 Arena on February 20 2010. Jimmy's typical reaction: "Thank gawd you didn't put on a candle for every year ... we could have started a new Great Fire of London."

times I mis-cued to the off-side I just had to surrender the runs. My partner thought I had gone quite potty."

Davd's greatest stunt was when he and John Morris buzzed the pitch in a hired Tiger Moth during the England innings against Queensland at Carrara during the 1990-91 tour. Gower's only regret is that he did not put the finishing touch to the operation. "We were going to shower the fielders with water bombs," David explained. "but our flying time was up and we were running out of fuel."

As the biplane flew low over the pitch, England batsmen Allan Lamb and Robin Smith looked up in amazement. Smith reacted by putting his bat to his shoulder and mimed taking rifle shots at the invader, not knowing it was his team-mates buzzing them. 'Biggles' Gower and Morris were each fined £1,000 by the MCC chiefs. In my opinion they should have given them medals for bringing a smile to the face of sport.'

Jimmy on an awards cock-up ...

'I was at an awards ceremony back in the 1960s after Lynn Davies had won the men's long jump gold medal for Britain at the Tokyo Olympics. He won an award but couldn't get along to collect it. The chairman of the sponsors announcing the awards told a celebrity-packed audience at the posh Park Lane hotel: "Lynn Davies unfortunately can't be with us, but we send her our love wherever she is!"

Terry Downes, then the world middleweight champion, was sitting at my table, and shouted out: "Give her a kiss from me when you find her!'

Jimmy on the racing king Lester Piggott ...

'One of my great heroes was Lester Piggott, who always had a huge following from England when he rode at Longchamp. His army of fans, who had come out on charter flights, celebrated heavily when he won the Arc de Triomphe on Alleged in 1977. One of his followers was poured on the flight for the homeward journey, and he was halfway across the Channel when he became sober enough to remember that he had driven out to Paris.

A wealthy racegoer once sat alongside Lester at an awards dinner. He had a monogrammed tie, his initials on his cufflinks and a gold watch with his name inscribed on it. Lester leant across and said to him: "You frightened of forgetting who you are?"

Although a man of few words because of his deafness in one ear, Lester was the king of the one-liners. Racing correspondent Peter O'Sullevan once said to him, 'A university up in Scotland has asked me to give them a talk. What would you say to them?'.

"Easy," said Lester, 'I'd tell them I've got the 'flu."•

Jimmy on the sledgehammer wit of Ian Botham ...

•That great Australian wicket-keeper Rodney Marsh used to try to upset the concentration of batsmen by saying to them as he crouched behind the stumps: "How's your wife and my kids?"

Ian Botham was ready for him during a Test match, and replied: "The wife's gorgeous, but the kids are retarded!"•

Jimmy on the golf tee

Golf has always been a hobby of mine, without it grabbing me by the balls so to speak, as in the case of The Saint, who lives and breathes it. My favourite golf story involves one of the great old masters, Arnold Palmer. During a PGA golf tournament a commentator offered an exclusive insight into Arnie's game. "One of the reasons Arnie is playing so well," he told viewers, "is that he has a superstition. Before each tee shot, his wife has to take out his balls and kiss them..."

There was a slight pause followed by: "Oh my God, what have I just said?"

It was Arnie Palmer who, when asked by a novice how he could get ten shots off his score, replied: "Get yourself a good eraser."•

Jimmy confessing to being converted

•Difficult to believe, I suppose, but rugby has taken over from my football as the game I most like to watch. A couple of lovely stories – Gareth Edwards listened with a straight face as Welsh team coach John Dawes outlined his plan to introduce codewords at a training session before a match against England.

"When you want the open-side flanker to make a break, the codeword should start with a 'P'," said Dawes. "If you want a break on the blind side, use a codeword beginning with 'S'"

He tossed the ball to master scrum-half Edwards, who put it into the scrum and shouted the codeword: "Psychology!"

Another funny story was told to me by that great idol of Irish rugby, Tony O'Reilly, who later became the billionaire boss of Heinz. He was playing in a match for Ireland against England at Twickenham during which Phil Horrocks-Taylor cleverly dummied his way past Irish stand-off Mick English to score a try. "Horrocks went this way," said O'Reilly, "Taylor went that way, and poor Mick was left holding the hyphen."**

Jimmy on keeping abreast of the times

•Remember that bird, Erica Roe, who did a famous headline-hitting streak at Twickenham? She was an impressively built girl. Big Bill Beaumont, who was then England skipper, told me that he was standing with his back to her, so didn't see her starting to run the length of the field. He said the first he knew of it was when scrum-half Steve Smith shouted, "Hey, Bill, there's a bird just run on with your bum on her chest."**

And here's a typical Greavsie joke to finish this funny old game section:

•It's the first day of school and the teacher thought she'd get to know the new children in her class by asking them their name and what their father does for a living.

The first little girl says: "My name is Daisy and my daddy is a publican."

The next little boy says: "I'm Anthony and my dad is an electrician."

Another boy says: "My name is Peter, and my father is a bank clerk."

Then one little boy, wriggling in his seat with embarrassment, says: "My name is Martin and my father, uh, cleans urinals for a living."

The teacher quickly changes the subject because she senses the boy's humiliation. Later in the school playground she quietly asks Martin if it was really true that his Dad cleans urinals for a living, prepared to tell him that he should not feel any shame.

Martin blushes as he confesses: "No, I'm sorry, my dad doesn't clean urinals He is a Premier League football referee and I was just too embarrassed to admit it"**

18: Jimmy and the Banks of England

TO get a feel of what it was like for Jimmy when he was emerging from the lost years we turn to an all-embracing chat that he had with his old friend Gordon Banks, another icon I am proud to represent. We decided to dive between the covers of Gordon's excellent first autobiography *Banks of England* and reproduce a riveting interview he had with Jimmy back in 1980. Their mutual mate Norman Giller was working the tape recorder:

'We had not seen each other for a couple of years and I was expecting the worst after all the harrowing stories I had heard and read about his drink problem. But as he came towards me, moving through the crowded hotel foyer with his familiar balance and economy of effort, I was pleasantly surprised. Jimmy Greaves looked a million dollars.

I had found it hard to believe when he had confessed publicly to being an alcoholic. He had certainly liked his drink in the days when we were England team-mates, but there were players with bigger consumption who had not suffered the nightmare Jimmy had lived through.

As we shook hands with a warmth that suddenly evaporated time and cemented our old friendship we took instant stock of each other. Jimmy wasted no time in getting his sharp Cockney wit to work.

"Just think, Gordon," he said, "since we last played for England together you've become one-eyed and I've become pie-eyed …!"

It was the old Greavsie smiling up at me. Mischievous, impish. A loveable little sod. I wanted to cuddle this lovely man who had given me and millions of football fans so much pleasure and fun over the years.

We were together in a London hotel to talk over old times. I had decided I needed help to revive old memories for my book, and who better, I thought, than Jimmy Greaves who just happened to be one of the greatest things on two feet during my playing career. We had shared so much together both on and off the pitch during the high summer of our playing days.

Now, with a tape-recorder between us, we looked back on the good old days and – sad to say – some not-so-good times …

GORDON: "The first time we were together, you bugger, you made me look a right bloody idiot! Can you remember it?"

GREAVSIE: "That must have been about 1959 or '60. You had been called up to the England Under-23 squad for the first time."

GORDON: "That's right. We were training at Stamford Bridge and the Press photographers wanted an action shot of me for their files. I asked you to kick the ball to me so that I could make a save. As you approached the ball you dipped your left shoulder and I dived to my right as you slipped the ball into the other corner of the net. The photographers fell about laughing."

GREAVSIE: "That was twenty years ago. Twenty years. It seems like only yesterday. I remember that we had two nicknames for you. One was Fernandel because you looked so much like the rubber-faced French comedian. The other was Sugar. You were always impersonating that entertainer who pretended to be drunk. What was his name …?"

GORDON: "Freddie Frinton. He used to sing Sugar in the Morning with a bent cigarette in his mouth and his top hat over his eyes."

GREAVSIE: "You used to have us in fits taking him off and staggering about as if you were drunk out of your head. So we called you Sugar. It might have been more appropriate if I'd done the drunk act!"

GORDON: "Actually, Jim, I admire the way you've stood up and faced your problem. It took a lot of courage admitting to the world you were an alcoholic."

GREAVSIE: "It was the only way I could beat the illness. I knew that with everybody's eyes on me my pride would help me conquer the problem. When I was asked to write an autobiography (*This One's On Me*) I decided to hang out my skeleton for public viewing. I used the book as a psychiatrist's couch and it did me the world of good."

GORDON: "I really used to envy you, did you know that, Jim? You seemed to have everything going for you. I admired the way you were able to cut off from your playing career to concentrate on building up a successful business. Everything seemed to come so easily to you on the football field and I thought all was perfect with your businesses and your marriage."

GREAVSIE: "I drank it all away. It got so that the booze became like a monster. To be honest, I'm lucky to be alive. But then, you've hardly had roses all the way since we last played together."

GORDON: "You can say that again. But, like you, I've had to come to terms with it. Out of the wreckage, we can salvage the self-satisfaction that we have both been able

It's the early 1980s and Gordon Banks and Jimmy reminisce on the fun they had when playing against each other. Get Jim's attempt at a perm!

to help others because of the nightmares we have experienced. I'm sure your book has given hope to a lot of people with the drink problem. Likewise, I have been able to give encouragement to many victims of accidents who have lost an eye. Particularly youngsters. Many parents have asked me to write to children who have lost the sight of an eye to tell them they can still lead ordinary lives."

GREAVSIE: "Something I've learned from the hell I've been through is that you can achieve anything you want provided you are single-minded about it."

GORDON: "Exactly. I made up my mind I was going to play again and I did. Admittedly it wasn't in top-grade football, but at least I got another couple of seasons in when everybody had given me up as finished."

GREAVSIE: "I could have wept for you when I heard about your car smash. In fact I went on a bender when I read about it. I was close to rock bottom with my drinking at the time and remember wondering why life had to be so cruel. You still had so much to give to the game. Goalkeeping is such an easy job that you all go on playing until it's time to collect your old age pension.

GORDON: "Very funny, Greavsie. You and I both know that it's the hardest of all jobs in football. Certainly in my time we used to get knocked to bits. But now 'keepers get the protection from referees that they deserve. But you're right in saying that I still had plenty more to give. I was looking forward to several more years at the top when I had my accident. That was obviously a terrible period in both our lives. I came pretty close to breaking down, but I got myself sorted out in America. It was just a question of getting away from domestic pressures for a while so that I could think everything through. Ursula was strong enough to cope with it and to understand that I was going through torture after the car crash. She and my kids were smashing, and we soon got our family unit back on track. It's been wonderful to be part of watching my children grow up. They give me so much pleasure."

GREAVSIE: "Well all I hope, Gordon, is that you let this tape go into the book verbatim, and tell it as it is. I'm sure people will admire you for the way you have managed to hold everything together despite all the problems. And I know what you mean by the enjoyment you get from being with your kids. Now that I've kicked the bottle I spend all my spare time at home with Irene and the kids, and we get on marvellously together. I call them kids! Lynn, my eldest daughter, has just got married."

GORDON: "Robert, my eldest, is talking about marriage. God, Jim, we could be grandfathers the next time we meet …"

We took a rest from our taping session to share a pot of tea. Joker Jim couldn't resist a gag at his own expense. "At least it's cheaper drinking with me these days, Gordon," he said. "A couple of years ago this reunion would have cost you a bottle of vodka!"

As Jimmy poured the tea, my mind was weighing up what he had said about "telling it as it is". How much should a sportsman strip himself for his public?

I went through torment in the months after the crash, and it was extremely tough on Ursula. Both of us could have capitalised by accepting big-money offers to tell our stories. But it was just not our way. We both believe that people in the public eye deserve their privacy.

Our marriage was strong enough to survive the sort of strains and stresses that have broken many others. Some rubbish found its way into the newspapers but the poison of publicity generated by the tabloid press could not break the bond of love between my family and myself, and once I had completed my contract in the United States I could not get back quickly enough to them.

My thoughts were broken by the sight of Jimmy almost choking over his teacup with laughter. "What have you remembered?" I asked, the tape recorder switched back on …

GREAVSIE: "Do you recall asking my advice about a transfer in 1967 when Leicester put you up for sale? There were two clubs in for you."

GORDON: "That's right, Liverpool and Stoke. I rang you to ask which of the clubs you would select."

GREAVSIE: "It's just come back to me what I said to you at the time. My advice was that you should go to Stoke because Liverpool were a finished force. With foresight like that I should have been a BBC weather forecaster."

GORDON: "That's right, you big pillock. Liverpool were such a finished force that they have since won every bloody thing in sight. Still, I've got no regrets about the move I made. Stoke were a great club to be with. They could play some cracking football and socially I would have to say they were the top club in the country. You would have had a ball with us, Jimmy."

GREAVSIE: "Yes, you had a good drinking school there. I've had lots of good nights out with you and my old mate George Eastham."

GORDON: "George was with us in the squad that night in 1964 when we nipped out for a drink in the West End the night before flying out for a match in Portugal."

GREAVSIE: "Alf (Ramsey) went potty. We thought we'd got away with it when we crept to our hotel rooms at about two o'clock in the morning without being spotted.

But trainer Harold Shepherdson had been to our rooms and put our passports on each of our beds. Let's think now. Who were the other players who went on the razzle with us?"

GORDON: "Apart from George, you and me there was Bobby Charlton, Ray Wilson, Budgie Byrne …"

GREAVSIE: "And don't forget our leader Bobby Moore, the man with the hollow legs. He could drink us all under the table, and then dance on it. Mooro and I were always getting each other in trouble with our love for a bevy."

GORDON: "What was the name of that bar we were drinking at?"

GREAVSIE: "The Beachcomber. They had all those exotic drinks, remember? We got stuck into a drink called a Zombie. It was a rum-based drink with a real kick."

GORDON: "That was the place with alligators in the tank. Ray Wilson kept lobbing chunks of ice out of the ice bucket at them."

GREAVSIE: "Nobody said a dicky bird to us the next morning, but when we got to Lisbon for our last training session Alf said in that exaggerated posh voice of his, 'I think there are seven gentlemen who wish to see me …'"

GORDON: "Alf was fuming. He left us in no doubt that he would never again tolerate us breaking curfews. He said he would have sent us all home if he'd had enough players in the squad. And he would have done as well. Alf was the most loyal bloke walking this earth if you gave him one hundred per cent, but anything less and he could cut you dead."

GREAVSIE: "A myth has been allowed to grow about Alf and me. People think we hated each other, when in fact we got on quite well. He could hit the old G and Ts when he was relaxed, and we had several good drinking sessions. Once switched off, he could be very humorous in a dry way, and had a warmth that unfortunately for him he failed to show in public."

GORDON: "Thank goodness, we won that match in Portugal. He picked all seven of we so-called rebels and we won 4-3 in an epic game."

GREAVSIE: "Two of the AWOL men, Budgie Byrne and Bobby Charlton scored the goals. Budgie helped himself to the sweetest of hat-tricks. Alf allowed himself quite a few G-and-Ts that night. Budgie could easily outpoint me in the elbow-raising game. Johnny was one of the greatest touch players I've ever played with. But for a knee injury, he would have been a cert for the 1966 World Cup squad. He's doing nicely for himself now down in South Africa. What a character."

GORDON: "We all felt for you when Alf left you out of the team for the World Cup final. You didn't say much, but we all knew you were sick."

GREAVSIE: "What could I say? The team had played magnificently against Portugal in the semi-final when I was nursing an injury. Alf had to decide whether to change the team and it was quite understandable when he stuck with a winning side. It was the worst thing that happened to me in my career, missing that final. I got well sozzled that night, and nipped off with my wife Irene for a holiday in the West Indies. The story got around that I had snubbed Alf and the after-match dinner, but I have always avoided those sort of things. I didn't want to become the story. England's victory deserved all the headlines. Anyway, Gordon, that's enough about me. This is supposed to be your book. I've got some statistics here that will interest you. According to the record books I played twenty-three League games against you and scored thirteen goals."

GORDON: "That should be fourteen goals. D'you remember that fantastic shot of yours on the turn at Leicester when you were in your early days with Spurs? I didn't get a sniff of the ball as it flashed into the net. It was right on half-time and we thought the ref had whistled for a goal, but then he said he'd blown for half-time and refused to allow the goal. All you Spurs players went berserk, and no wonder, because it was a belter of a goal."

GREAVSIE: "Here are some more statistics, Gordon, which incidentally come from my well researched book. Ends commercial! You and I played together in twenty matches for England between 1963 and 1967, and we were on the losing side only three times."

GORDON: "Our first defeat was against Scotland in our first game together. That bugger Jim Baxter took control of the game and scored both their goals. I thought he was going to become the greatest Scottish footballer of all time, but he didn't maintain his standards."

GREAVSIE: "It's no secret that Baxter had my trouble. He preferred a glass in his hand to a ball at his feet. But what a player when he was at his peak! He was as smooth as silk and all style and skill. They murdered us in midfield where they had Dave Mackay and John White as well as Slim Jim Baxter. The only midfield trio to match them was the one we had in the Spurs side of the time – Danny Blanchflower, Mackay and dear John White."

GORDON: "They were a bit special. Just my luck to come up against them in my international debut. And that Spurs midfield trio was as good as there has ever been in club football."

The pipe of peace for Jimmy as he golfs during a 1960s England training get-together

GREAVSIE: "I thought your international career was finished the next month. Do you remember, we played Brazil?"

GORDON: "Of course, I bloody remember. How could I forget that free-kick of Pepe's? It did a circular tour of the penalty area before going past me into the net."

GREAVSIE: "I never saw Alf get so boiled up over anything. He kept saying over and over again that he had warned you to watch out for that bender. In fact he went on so much about it that in the end every time he mentioned it we would fall about laughing behind his back and poke faces at you."

GORDON: "I still insist that no ball has ever bent as much as that one. It would have taken Superman to save it. Alf wouldn't have it, though."

GREAVSIE: "Let's be honest, Gordon, you were positioned behind the wall instead of to the right of it."

GORDON: "Now don't you start, Greavsie. Even now I can hear Alf saying that in my sleep. I wondered if he would drop me for it, but I kept my place for the first tour match against Czechoslovakia."

GREAVSIE: "That was the game when Alf told us we had to get back to the hotel immediately after the game. I was elected spokesman and had to ask if it would be all right for us to go out for a quiet drink before going back. He gave that piercing look of his and said: 'If you must have a drink you can go back to the f***** hotel and have it."

GORDON: "Alf didn't swear very often, but when he did you knew he meant what he was saying. As I remember it, we did go straight back to the hotel that night and Alf and all the officials joined us in a big party to celebrate what had been a great 4-2 victory."

GREAVSIE: "Everybody felt like death the next morning and we had to fly to East Germany. It was a diabolical flight because we had to go through the Berlin corridor at about 3,000 feet and the plane was pitching about like a rowing boat in a storm. I was sitting with Bobby Moore and he said all straight-faced, 'We'll be all right because we've got the England doctor to look after us.' He pointed across the aisle and there was Doc Bass (Dr Alan Bass) laid flat out with sweat pouring off him and looking as green as the Wembley turf. It was a mixture of a hangover and the flight. Mooro called out, 'Is there a doctor on board for the doctor …'?"

GORDON: "Wasn't it in East Germany that Alf took us all to the pictures to see what he said would be an English film?"

GREAVSIE: "It was an English-made war film and Alf said it would be in English with German subtitles."

GORDON: "That's right. When the film started we could not believe our ears. The English actors were talking with dubbed-in German voices. We started having a moan at Harold Shep who kept saying, 'In about five or ten minutes' time they start speaking in English.' When they did start speaking in another language it was Russian and they put up sub-titles in German. With that we all got up en bloc and walked out of the cinema."

GREAVSIE: "Talking of doing things en bloc, d'you remember when we were sitting on the touchline watching Brazil play Argentina in Sao Paulo in 1964? The crowd started pelting us with rubbish and Alf gave the shortest tactical talk of his life, 'Run, lads.'"

GORDON: "I was sitting next to Alf and his actual words after a juicy apple core had splattered against his back were: 'I don't know abut you, gentlemen, but I'm f***** off!'"

GREAVSIE: "Do you realise, Gordon, that we were on the losing side in our first and last matches together for England and each time it was against the Scots."

GORDON: "The second time was in 1967. We lost 3-2 at Wembley. It was our first defeat since the World Cup and the Scots had the cheek to claim they were the world champions."

GREAVSIE: "I've got painful memories of that match. I got a knock on an ankle that put me out for two weeks. Jack Charlton broke a toe and moved up to centre-forward and Ray Wilson was a hobbling passenger for most of the game. I got some terrible stick in the Press for my performance, but if they had seen the state of my ankle after the game I think they would have been more sympathetic."

GORDON: "I could never understand why Alf didn't recall you after that match. He said a couple of years later that you had asked not to be selected."

GREAVSIE: "Alf had that all wrong. I would loved to have got my England place back, but Alf had misunderstood a conversation we once had. He had been getting into the habit of calling me up for training with the squad and then not picking me for the match. You know me, Gordon, I was hardly the world's greatest trainer. I'm the bloke who once got fined by Spurs for taking a lift on a milkfloat during a cross country fitness run. Anyway, I told Alf that unless I was going to play I preferred to give the training get-togethers a miss. He interpreted that as meaning I didn't want to play for England any more."

We stopped talking while Jimmy ordered another pot of tea. "I'm hooked on this stuff now," he said. "I drink gallons of tea and coffee, but at least when I wake up the next morning I don't have a hangover and I know exactly what I did the previous day."

You could not tell by looking at him the hell he had been through. He was elegantly dressed and appeared prosperous. Since we'd last played together he had grown a thick, Mexican-style moustache and his hair was well groomed in the modern bubble-cut fashion. I noticed that he smoked heavily, but even in his playing days with England he had liked a cigarette or pipe.

People who had not been lucky enough to have seen him at his peak missed the pleasure of watching a genius at work. I always used to enjoy playing against him because it was such a challenge, and if you were ever beaten by him (which I often was) then at least you had the consolation of knowing a master had put the ball past you.

We continually chatted to each other during games and Jimmy used to tell me exactly where he was going to place his shots. Of course he was bluffing and he would have me diving the wrong way.

As he sat there, teapot in hand, I wondered what his modern-day transfer value would be if Trevor Francis could fetch the first million-pounds fee. It seemed a good point at which to switch the tape recorder back on …

GORDON: "If Trevor Francis is worth a million, Jim, I reckon you would have been worth at least twice that at your peak."

GREAVSIE: "Careful, Gordon. People will read that and think we have formed a mutual-admiration society. Funnily enough, I was just going to say to you if Phil Parkes is worth half a million then your value would be somewhere in excess of three million. I don't mean that as a slight on Phil, because he's an excellent goalkeeper, but I have never seen anybody to match you for class and consistency."

GORDON: "This is getting embarrassing. Let's change the subject. Would you like to be playing in today's game or were you happy to have had your peak when you did?"

GREAVSIE: "Obviously I would like the money they are earning now, but I would not want to swap eras. I think you and I were lucky to have played when we did. I am sure the game was more enjoyable for players and spectators, particularly in the late 1950s and early 1960s."

Jimmy presents Cloughie with a Manager of the Month award

GORDON: "I agree with you. Goalkeepers got little or no protection from the referee when I first came into the game, and the likes of Bobby Smith and Nat Lofthouse thought nothing of trying to batter you into the net. But it was accepted as part and parcel of the game and you just took it in your stride. Now I think if anything goalkeepers are over protected and consequently they are not learning the physical aspect of the game. It's definitely not as entertaining for spectators to watch."

GREAVSIE: "The last time I played with you, Gordon, was in a Goaldiggers match for the Playing Fields Fund. It was some time after your accident and Jimmy Hill had arranged the game against a team of European All Stars at Birmingham. Bobby Robson was playing in midfield and you – if you'll pardon the expression – were having a blinder, stopping everything that came at you. Bobby turned to me and said: 'If Banksie is one-eyed then all I can say is that the First Division has a load of blind goalkeepers.' After the match he told me he was going to try to sign you for Ipswich, but nothing came of it."

GORDON: "That's the story of my life since the accident. Promises, promises. I got really disillusioned trying to get back into the game. Clubs just didn't want to know me. I don't know if they think I've lost the power to think as well as to see out of one eye, but some clubs didn't even have the decency to reply to my job applications."

GREAVSIE: "It's astonishing how many of that 1966 World Cup squad are now out of the game. Ronnie Springett and Peter Bonetti were the other two goalkeepers in the squad. They are both out. The full-backs were George Cohen, Ray Wilson, Jimmy Armfield and Gerry Byrne. They're all out."

GORDON: "Even Mooro is out of the game. It's madness. Surely the Football Association could employ him in some capacity. All that knowledge going to waste. I would have jumped at the chance to take over the England youth team after Brian Clough and Peter Taylor said they were no longer interested. But I didn't get a look-in."

GREAVSIE: "Nobby and Jackie are managers, but they are the only two unless you count Geoff Hurst, who's involved with the England team. So out of twenty-two players, thirteen of them are no longer connected with the game at top level. Ron Flowers, Roger Hunt, John Connelly, Terry Paine, George Eastham and even Bobby Charlton are not involved in the League scene."

GORDON: "Only Norman Hunter, Ballie, Martin Peters and Ian Callaghan are still playing in the League. I wonder if any of them will get the chance to manage or coach a top club? Or have they got disillusionment to come like so many others who were in that 1966 squad?"

GREAVSIE: "I've never wanted to get involved in the game as a manager. There are too many pressures for my liking. You are answerable to too many people, most of whom don't know what day it is. You have to satisfy not only your players and interfering directors but also the fans and the media. If you're lucky, you might find a few minutes each day for your family. That's not for me. It would be enough to drive me to drink."

GORDON: "Then how do you see the future, Jim? I love being involved in football and want to try to give back all the things that I have learned about the game. How can you live without it?"

GREAVSIE: "Things are opening up for me in the media. I have a column in *The Sun* and I am starting to get a lot of work in front of the television cameras. That's the way I want to go … telling footballers and managers what they are doing wrong without any of the responsibility of having to put it right!"

As I watched Jimmy walk jauntily away through the crowded hotel foyer, weaving easily past people as if they were not there, the years melted away and I could see a little white-shirted imp conjuring his way through defences for goals that had even the opposition applauding in appreciation. Jimmy Greaves. They don't make them like him anymore.**'**

It's astonishing to realise that this interview comes from 1980, and so many of the opinions Gordon and Greavsie held then hold up today. The thought of Jimmy with a bubble perm is about as funny as it gets.

Now from the greatest goalkeeper of them all on to a series of tributes from the great footballers who played with and against Jimmy ...

Author plug: I have written a book with Pele and Gordon called *BANKS v PELE, The Save That Shook the World.* You can order autographed copies from our website at www.a1sportingmemorabilia.co.uk Ends commercial :-)

DAVE MACKAY

❛I hate to admit it as a Scot, but Jimmy was the greatest British goal scorer of my life time – or anybody else's for that matter. My countryman Denis Law was a bit special, but Jimmy was more prolific. It was a joy to play with him, even though he could be a lazy so-and-so. I'll always remember his first goal for us, a spectacular scissors kick after Terry Medwin had nodded on my long throw. I thought to myself, "Aye, he'll do for us!" For all his ability, there is not a boastful bone in his body and I think the world of him.❜

SIR GEOFF HURST

❛It's history how I took Jimmy's place in the World Cup after he got injured, and made a bit of a name for myself with my hat-trick in the final. It speaks volumes for the sort of bloke Jimmy is that he has never ever let it get between us. We have remained good pals, and get involved in business deals and stage shows promoted by A1 Sporting Speakers. I was a completely different type of player to Jim, and I was in awe of the way he could dismantle even the tightest defence with his skill. He was simply the best.❜

PETER BONETTI

‘Jimmy and I were kids together at Chelsea, and I always maintain that was when he was at his best. His early performances for Chelsea were mind-blowing. It's part of his legend how he convinced Billy Wright he should hang up his boots after he had scored five goals against a Wolves team that dominated football at the time. He was like greased lightning, and used to unbalance defenders with his speed and dribbling skill. After many of his goals you would find at least three defenders on their bums wondering what had happened. He was a nightmare for goalkeepers to face because he was never predictable with his finishing. He had the knack of passing rather than shooting the ball into the net. A pure genius.’

MARTIN PETERS

‘I idolised Jimmy when I was a kid. He was three years older than me, and I remember him playing for his school side against ours and scoring eleven goals in a 13-0 victory. It was surreal when I moved to Tottenham, with Jimmy going to West Ham as a £54,000 makeweight. At his peak he was worth his weight in gold, or perhaps that should be goals. We all felt sick for him when he missed out on the World Cup final, because you would have put all your money on him being part of it. They say that started him on the booze but Jimmy always liked a pint and he admits that his problem was nothing to do with the World Cup. All of us in the game are lost in admiration for the way he beat his problem, and what he's achieved since.’

CLIFF JONES

'He was a Cockney cheeky chappie, who was always good for a laugh on and off the pitch. I remember him taking a ride on a milk float during a pre-season training run. He was probably the worst trainer ever, but give him a ball on the pitch and he was suddenly the greatest thing on two feet. Some of his goals were out of this world, and I often found myself applauding like a spectator. But for Jim all goals were the same, whether following an amazing dribbling run or just tapped in from six inches. The only thing that mattered to him was getting the ball into the net. He was a born goal scorer. I couldn't believe it when Alf Ramsey left him out of the World Cup team. England's best player was reduced to a spectator.'

MARTIN CHIVERS

'I was privileged to play with Jimmy at the back end of his career with Tottenham. We were never really given the time to perfect our act, but there were moments when I discovered just what a genius he was. He had a deceptive change of pace and could send defenders tumbling by a sudden spurt and then a change of direction. I have seen few players able to match his close ball control. Just as I thought we were starting to click he was off to West Ham. I would liked to have played with him longer, because there is no doubt that he is one of the all-time greats. It is incredible what he has done since retiring, beating the bottle then having a great TV career and now a very funny stand-up comedian. He has lived three lives in one.'

BOBBY SMITH

'Jim and I have a laugh when we see what the players are earning these days. If he had been at his peak now the bidding would have to start at £50 million. We had a great understanding. I used to knock 'em down, and Jim would knock 'em in. I am not boasting, but anybody who saw us will confirm there were about three years when we were the best double act in the game. He was an unselfish player and was just as happy to see me banging the ball into the net. I was all power, Jim was all skill. Defenders just did not know how to handle us. I remember when we knocked nine goals into the Scotland net, with Dave Mackay and Denis Law spitting blood. Jimmy got a hat-trick and I scored two. That was as good as it gets.'

RON 'CHOPPER' HARRIS

'I am proud to say I was one of the few defenders who could stop Jimmy playing ... well, for at least 89 minutes of the match. Then the little sod would give me the slip and grab a goal with his only chance. We often appear on stage together these days, and Jim tells the audience I am a bruise on his memory. I was allowed to tackle from behind in those days, and I always liked to let Jimmy know I was there. Once I was sticking closer to Jim than a second skin, and he said, 'Chop, you'd come to the loo if I went for a sh*t.' I told him, 'No, Jim, but I'd be waiting for you when you came out.' Let me go on record as saying he was the greatest goal scorer I ever marked ... take that how you like. Seriously, he was the best of them all.'

DENIS LAW

'Both Jimmy and I felt we were prisoners in Italy. I was playing with Joe Baker in Turin, and like Jimmy we got to hate their defensive style of football. It was wonderful to get back to the freedom of the English game, and Jim really filled his boots. No question that he was the greatest goal scorer England ever produced. I recall a match when he played for England against the Rest of the World, and he was the best player on the pitch by a mile. He scored the winning goal and would have had four but for Russian goalkeeper Lev Yashin. I scored the Rest of the World's goal and said to Jimmy at the end, "You should have had a hat-trick. It's a bit easier than in Italy." He agreed, and said: "Anything is easier than in Italy."'

DON HOWE

'I played in the England team in Peru when Jimmy made his international debut, and his goal was one of the few bright things on that South American tour. He became one of our all-time great forwards, and I remember us having sunburned tongues when he scored five goals against West Brom in a club game in his Chelsea days. When I went into management I often used to wish I had a Jimmy Greaves to call on, but that was an impossible dream. Jimmy was unique, and he could literally make a goal out of nothing. I considered it an honour to be on the same pitch as him, and it has been a delight to see all that he has achieved since hanging up his boots and having that little local difficulty with alcohol.'

PAT JENNINGS

'I grew up thinking Jimmy was a genius because of the number of goals he scored against Nothern Ireland, and when I joined him at Spurs I found no reason to change my rating of him. He was a magician with the ball at his feet, a different style of player to my Irish idol George Best but sometimes more effective at the way he could cut through a defence. We had a great laugh in 1967 when I scored with a clearance that went first bounce over the head of Alex Stepney in the Man United goal in the Charity Shield. He turned to Alan Gilzean and said, 'D'you realise, Gilly, this makes Pat our top scorer.' Greavsie and Gilly were a fantastic combination. They would be worth a fortune in today's transfer market.'

STEVE PERRYMAN

'When I broke into the Tottenham team at the age of 17, Jimmy was just beginning to wind down but he was still as good a striker as there was in the League. He would wander around seemingly not much interested in what was going on around him and then, suddenly, he would pounce on a pass and with a clever change of pace and direction he would send defenders into a blind panic on his way to scoring a goal from out of nowhere. Not only was he one of the greatest ever footballers, but he is also a lovely bloke. His stand-up comedy act is as good as you will see from a professional comedian, and there's not a programme on TV today to touch the *Saint and Greavsie* shows for a mix of comedy and serious football stuff.'

EXTRA-TIME: Jimmy's fan mail

WE asked Jimmy Greaves fans to e-mail us with memories of watching their hero play. It is nearly 40 years since Jimmy kicked a ball in League fooball, but his dazzling feet and feats live on in the minds of those lucky enough to have seen him in action. Here are a cross-section of the memories submitted to us, exclusively for this *Jimmy Greaves at 70* book:

THE MOMENT I WAS HOOKED

KEITH PRESTON, Romford

'Greavsie is the main reason I became a Spurs supporter. Though my dad tried his hardest to make me a West Ham fan, once I had seen Greavsie in action he had no chance. I was allowed to watch my first live F.A. Cup final live in 1962, the 3-1 win over Burnley. When Jim scored after just three minutes I was hooked, and straight after the game I was in our back garden recreating his goal. Kids, huh! It took two years of hard work pestering a staunch West Ham fan to take me to White Hart Lane to see my new hero. I finally broke him down and he took me to my first live game at The Lane. It was our last home game of the 1963-64 season, and I wasn't disappointed as Jimmy scored the only goal of the game. His partnership with Alan Gilzean was as close to perfect as you could get. Thanks Jimmy for the great memories.'

HIS GOALS WILL NEVER BE SURPASSED

JOHN MacCABE, Poplar

'Apart from being the most prolific goalscorer I have seen or am ever likely to see in a Spurs shirt I have three very distinct memories of the third greatest Spur ever (behind Dave Mackay and Danny Blanchflower).

First his goal against Glasgow Rangers direct from a corner in the Cup Winners' Cup in 1962, secondly running past Harry Redknapp and catching hold of his hand with a big grin on his face just before a free kick when we stuffed West Ham 5 - 1 in 1967, and lastly the great goal he scored against Forest in the semi-final at Hillsborough in April 1967. Greavesie's ability to pass the ball into the back of the net with such ease, accuracy and regularity will never be surpassed and will ever live in the memory of myself and thousands of other true Lilywhites who were there to witness such events.'

THAT FIRST UNFORGETTABLE GOAL

TIM DAVIS, Notting Hill

'It is hard to believe that it is almost 50 years since Jimmy Greaves played his first match for Spurs and I am just chuffed to be able to say that I was there at White Hart Lane to see it. Jimmy had played his first ever League game at the Lane in 1957 - for Chelsea - and he started a habit of scoring in debut games that he never stopped as Chelsea drew 1-1 with Tottenham.

Now it was four years on and he was being brought back by Bill Nicholson from an unhappy short sojourn in Milan to be the goal-scoring icing on the Double-Winning team cake. Spurs were playing Blackpool in the First Division and for once everything else seemed subservient to what Greaves would do in this game and whether he could perpetuate his phenomenal record of scoring a goal in his first game for a new team.

What I recall most vividly about the day was the feeling of anticlimax as in the first 25 minutes of the match the great man barely had a touch. Then Dave Mackay's throw-in was nodded on by Terry Medwin at about waist height. There was a white blur as Jimmy launched himself horizontal to the ground and, instantaneously, the ball crashed into the back of the net. The speed of his reflexes had been staggering and it took a split second before the crowd appreciated just what he had done. The whole place then went potty saluting the sheer brilliance of what had just been witnessed.

As is well known, Jimmy proceeded to score a hat-trick in that first game for Spurs and the team ran out 5-2 winners over Blackpool. He went on to score many more remarkable goals for Tottenham but it was that first one that told us all that we were fortunate in the extreme to have a genius in our midst.'

THE JUNIOR DAYS OF GREAVES AND CLISS

RICHARD GRANT, Sydney, Australia, via West Hendon

'My best memory of Greavsie was his first game hat-trick at The Lane and particularly the left footed scossors kick into the roof of the net. He probably should have headed it, but in todays parlance, he really didn't "do" headers. So he gets his body horizontal, several feet off the ground and kicks it instead.

I'm three years younger than Jimmy and when I was about 13 we lived in West Hendon, just off the Edgware Road near the Welsh Harp lake. In those days there was a pub with the same name on the Edgware Road near the North Circular Road and a slightly hilly football pitch above it. Chelsea Juniors sometimes used that ground on Saturday mornings and my Dad and I used to walk down to watch the games, although neither of us were Chelsea supporters I might add. It's a bit hazy now and I can't be sure whether we had to pay or get a vantage point on the hill outside the ground. Probably the latter. Anyway, I think that is the first time I saw Jimmy play. He was outstanding then, and they also had a player called David Cliss who was equally talented at that age, but, like Tommy Harmer, was a bit lightweight for those times given the muddy pitches and the heavy leather footballs. We did not hear much more of Cliss, but Jimmy became a legend. It was great to be in at the start.'

A GOAL FITTING FOR THE TATE GALLERY

STUART ELLISON, Sydney, Australia, via Brighton

'Having seen many exciting games involving Greavsie the one memory that stands out more than others was our home game against Man Utd in 1965. On that particular day my mother was unable to go to the game, so I was able to give her ticket to my school friend Nick Tate, who like myself was 12 years old and football mad but at that time was a Man Utd supporter.

The atmosphere at the ground was, as usual, electric. Everytime Jimmy was about to take one of his trademark inswinging corners the crowd in the stands would be stamping their feet, creating an incredible sound likened to a runaway train going through the stands. On that day we not only witnessed a 5-1 hammering of a Man Utd side featuring the likes of Charlton, Law and Best but we saw what I still consider one of the greatest individual goals

Greaves collected the ball in his own half, went past four defenders and the 'keeper before "passing" the ball into the net. A truly memorable goal and made more memorable by the fact from that day on Nick, who is still a very close friend after 45 years, became an avid Spurs fan and still following the Spurs today. Indeed last year I went back to the UK from Sydney and went to the Spurs v Man United Carling Cup Final with Nick. Unfortunately the result wasn't the same as in 1965!'

TURNING DEFENDERS INTO COCO THE CLOWNS

DON MAHONEY, Potters Bar

'I was just a young whipper snapper when the legend that was Jimmy Greaves was making the best defenders around look like they were auditioning as Coco the Clown stand ins. The best compliment I have ever heard other than he was the greatest was that if he had played in the World Cup final then England would have won without the need of extra time! I saw a picture of one of his goals taken from behind the goal – the view was like a group of drunken men on a stag night trying to get up off the floor in a daze. Pure magic.'

THE MAN OF GENESIS WHO THINKS JIMMY IS A GENIUS
PHIL COLLINS

'When I was a boy, there was only one footballer I wanted to meet, only one player I wanted to be .... Jimmy Greaves. I supported Spurs from a distance in Hounslow. I never went to White Hart Lane as it was too far for a youngster, but I followed every kick and every goal through the radio, on TV and in the newspapers.

Many years later I was fortunate to be given an award by the Variety Club, and when they invited me along I asked where I would be sitting. They went through the guest list with me, and when they said Saint and Greavsie would be there collecting an award, I said; "I'll only come if I can sit next to my hero Jimmy Greaves!"

I did go, I did sit next to Jimmy and we became pals. I would just like to say to him: 'Jimmy, you ARE and always will be my hero, lots of love and luck on reaching the seventies.'

THE FAGIN OF THE PENALTY AREA
IAN NOBLE, Canada via Chingford

❛The greatest goalscorer and scorer of great goals our club has ever had, or indeed ever likely to have. Geoffrey Green, legendary *Times* football writer, described him as the Fagin of the penalty area and that was a great comment. He could pick a defender's pocket and the guy would not even have known he was there.

Scorer of great goals and of all types of goals, not too many with his head granted; a joy to watch and we marvelled at his speed off the mark, intelligent running and supreme close ball control, and in my opinion still the best player I have ever seen in a one to one situation with only the goalkeeper to beat. It sounds easy but it is one of the hardest facets of the game to master. You could bet your life Jimmy would round the keeper and pass the ball into the net 99 times out of a 100.

I met him once at his old sports shop in Chingford and he was all that you hope your heroes will turn out to be if ever you meet them, modest unassuming and very amusing. Thanks, Jimmy, for all the wonderful memories you have given to Spurs fans over the years.❜

GENTLEMAN JIM AND THE GREATEST GOAL OF THEM ALL
ANDY NICHOLSON, North Petherton, Somerset

❛Jimmy Greaves will forever be my all time favourite player for Spurs and England. I remember getting his autograph for the first time in the late 60's and being totally overcome with ecstasy and joy. His was the one I always desired the most and after years of trying to get that elusive squiggle of the biro it's been treasured ever since. He had his moments, when the "small sherries" rather took over his life, and he once sported a terrible bubble perm, but he was always Gentleman Jim and his goal against Leicester at the Lane in 1968 was for everyone who witnessed it quite the greatest individual goal ever.

Sadly this was in the days when few matches were committed to film, but I can still, from the vantage of being midway up the Shelf on the half way line, picture the line of around five to six Foxes players all left in a trail on their backsides as Jimmy ran from immediately below me on the touchline, on the diagonal, towards the Paxton Road end, before finally beating a young Peter Shilton all ends up to pass the ball into the goal. No one did it better before or since. There's a great picture in my scrapbook of Jimmy calmly slotting the ball home with all the defenders left in his wake in different stages of getting to their feet, each with a look of complete bewilderment; priceless.❜

Note from Norman Giller: That goal against Leicester has been picked by many fans as Jimmy's greatest, rivalled by his wonder strike against Manchester United in 1965. I was reporting the Leicester match for the Daily Express. *A car accident delayed me, and as I ran up the steps to the Press box there was an enormous roar and Jimbo was wheeling away from goal, with a queue of Leicester players on their arses. It was the greatest goal I never saw ... and no TV cameras. Shilts always calls it the finest goal scored against him. I interviewed just about anybody who was anybody, including Bill Nick, who said in his succinct way: "It was very special." All Greavsie would say was: "It will teach you to drive properly ..." This is how Paul Smith, who runs the exceptionally informative www.spursodyssey.com website, remembers it:*

THE START OF MY SPURS ODYSSEY
PAUL SMITH, Sheffield

"On Saturday October 5th, 1968, there were no television cameras at White Hart Lane, but the 16-year-old Paul Smith was one of the lucky 36, 622 souls present. Spurs were playing Leicester and even those Leicester fans present would have applauded one of James P. Greaves' three goals that day. Leicester's goalkeeper was a very young Peter Shilton, who had not long succeeded Gordon Banks in goal. I was in the Park Lane End, sadly at the wrong end of the ground, and had to view this particular slice of history from behind the little magician we idolised as "Greavsie".

Jimmy picked up the ball near the half-way line and jinked all the way to goal, leaving about half a dozen Leicester defenders flailing in his trail, before sliding the ball past Shilton for a sensational goal. Match of the Day cameras did see a goal against Manchester United, which is heralded as one of Jimmy Greaves's greatest goals, but those of us at White Hart Lane for that Leicester game know that WE saw his best ever.

Spurs won 3-2 that day, but to be honest sometimes I'd see us lose, but be happy if I saw my all-time football hero Jimmy Greaves score for my beloved Spurs. I was also lucky enough to be in the ground on different days when he scored his 200th League goal for Spurs, and also (on another date) his 300th League goal. The standing ovations seemed to last for about five minutes.

Back to 5th October, 1968 and if you are lucky, you might find a photograph taken of the moment that Shilton was beaten. In the background you can see some of those defenders that Greaves had left on the ground picking themselves up. It was a condition that defenders often found themselves in after being passed by Greavsie. I was off on my Spurs Odyssey!"

HE WAS THE MASTER OF WEIGHTING A BALL
STEVE ALDERSON, Harlow

'The buzz around White Hart Lane whenever Greavsie picked the ball up within 35 yards of goal was amazing. I was a 10-year-old lad but still noticed the men in the stands take their hands out of their pockets in anticipation, ready to applaud another mazy run, or a ball bent with accuracy that we had only witnessed from the Brazilians, or just a simple tap in. We knew what Jimmy could do because we had seen it so many times before

Watching Greavsie's magical first touch, short burst of speed and sublime finishing leaving defenders with hands on hips blaming each other for losing him is a sight that I'll never forget.

In full flow he was unstoppable, not bullish like Rooney, or flamboyant like Ronaldo. He just had the knack of putting enough weight on a ball to take it away from defenders yet still be in total control of it himself.

What would a modern day Greavsie fetch on the transfer market today? Probably only three clubs in Erope that could afford him. You can study the facts and figures all you like but to have seen him contribute to them was a privilege. I take great pride in telling any one interested that I have seen the greatest goalscorer to pull on the white shirts of Spurs and England.'

A TRUE, NATURAL FOOTBALLING GENIUS
ADRIAN MURPHY, Hackney

'In this day of the mechanical footballer it is just a pleasure to look back at a natural footballer who was arguably the best in the world in his time. My dear mum, Patricia Murphy, loved him. And his famous pie and pint before games stories are wonderful and add to his legend. A true genius at his trade. I am writing this soon after watching Kranjcar score a classic goal for Tottenham at Stoke, following a clever step-over by Eidur Gudjohnsen. I am told this is the sort of football Greavsie was always producing when in partnership with Alan Gilzean. The are part of Tottenham's footballing folklore.'

SIX OF THE BEST FROM GREAVSIE
DAVID SIMMONS, Toronto via Finchley

'I can recall six occasions where Jimmy Greaves left me with a memory:
1. I was a young lad, in the early '60s, taken by my Dad to see the Spurs. We had endured a 0-0 draw against Sheffield United, and the next game to which we went was against Liverpool – and Jimmy scored, final scoreline 1-0. What was disconcerting is that I was unaware of the difference between the decorum

at the First team games v the Reserve team games. I was unaware that at the former, it was normal to get up and cheer, when a goal was scored, so I saw only a fraction of the goal and aftermath as the rows in front, well aware of the niceties involved, rose up, leaving me staring at a wall of coats and rear ends.

2. I remember watching an interview of Jimmy by the newly-minted football interviewer, Danny Blanchflower, now retired from playing. Interviews back then were serious affairs, but somehow Jimmy Greaves was not going to play ball (as it were). These interviews were more of a staged event, with technology in its infancy and a sequence of TV footage showing the Spurs 1962 F.A. Cup side emerging on to the Wembley pitch, for the second-half, was to be run. Danny asked Jimmy to describe what we were all seeing on the clip. Jimmy said something to the effect of "and there you are, and that's me helping you onto the pitch for the second-half." The 14 years older Blanchflower looked mortified, and for once the loquacious Irishman was lost for words.

3. Although we are accused of a surfeit of football on 'the box' nowadays, I can recall a Young England v. a Football League XI being shown. Jimmy Greaves and Terry Paine, for Young England, took the other team apart.

4. I can remember another interview with Jimmy, approaching the end of his career, with non-League Barnet. He was asked as to which of all the goals he scored, which one gave him the most satisfaction. He answered something to the effect of "the one last week, where the goalkeeper was bending down to do up his bootlace and I put it into the net, without him being aware."

5. Given the last comment, it is hardly surprising that when the time came for Spurs to put on a Testimonial for Jimmy, against the then top draw team Feyenoord, Jimmy got himself on the scoresheet, early on, by taking the ball j-u-s-t onside, and while Feyenoord were appealing, he scored.

6. The Football Annual that started out as "The Rothman's Football Yearbook" had a section, in one of the first two issues, devoted to the retiring Jimmy Greaves scoring record. They've never done that for any other player.

HOW MANY WOULD HE HAVE SCORED TODAY?
ROBERT ROCKETT, Maidenhead

‘It has been proved beyond argument that Jimmy Greaves was the greatest goal scorer ever for Tottenham in a day when the pitches were mudheaps, and he was being marked by the likes of Bite Yer Legs Hunter, Toothless Tiger Nobby Stiles and Chopper Harris! I wonder how many goals he would have scored today? I saw him close to the end of his career – scoring for West Ham at Tottenham!’

OH FOR A TIME MACHINE!

TOBY BENJAMIN, Brighton

❛I am too young to have watched Jimmy play but it is obvious from the records and all that is said and written about him that he was the greatest goal scorer Spurs have ever had. I wish I had a time machine to go back to the sixties and see him in action. I think the greatest testament to Jimmy is that I have seen around a hundred 'best ever' Spurs teams' posted on various message boards and he features in almost every team. It's as if the memory of his goals still permeate White Hart Lane all these years later.❜

YOUTUBE EVIDENCE OF THE GREAVES GREATNESS

ROB WOOLMER, New Zealand via Becontree

❛Jimmy is simply a legend, both for Tottenham and England. Such a shame he didn't play in the final of the World Cup – he would have graced that stage. What I would like to do for those not lucky enough to have seen him (and to refresh the memories of those who have) is point you to some remarkable footage on YouTube. Go here: www.youtube.com and then in the search box type in Greaves Spurs-Manchester United 1965. You are in for a feast.❜

THIS WAS EVEN BETTER THAN MARADONA

ALAN PAPWORTH, London

❛Jimmy's goal against Manchester United in 1965 was a bit special, but it was surpassed by the one he collected against Leicester City three years later. He collected a punt from goalkeeper Pat Jennings near the halfway line and close to The Shelf side of the pitch. He brought the ball instantly under control, turned his marker and embarked on a diagonal run, beating five players and slipping it past goalkeeper Peter Shilton at the Paxton End without a care in the world. I was there that day and it remains the greatest goal I have ever had the pleasure to have seen from anybody (even beating Maradona's second in the World Cup against England). The great pity was that is was not captured on film. It would still be showing weekly now because it was that incredible. Apparently, Greavsie can hardly remember it. Goals came so easily and naturally to this little genius.❜

RESPECTED AS THE GREATEST BY A GOONER

KEN RYAN, Brisbane, Australia, via North London

❛I grew up in a family full of six Arsenal supporters and my father admitted until the day he died that Jimmy Greaves was the greatest goal scorer he ever saw. He said that Greaves and George Best were the most feared opponents to visit Highbury. This is a pretty big statement and testament coming from a man who hated us Yids with a passion. Jimmy was not only a legend of the Lane but of the entire Beautiful Game.'

GREETINGS FROM THE TVam COUCH
LINDA RODRIGUEZ, Epping

'My Dad, a publican from Bethnal Green, took me to my first football match to watch Spurs. We were living in Blackpool at the time, so it was at Bloomfield Road and I remember us watching Jimmy getting on the coach afterwards. Dad thought Jimmy was the greatest footballer ever. Now fast forward ...

I wanted to get my daughter's birthday mentioned on TVam in 1986, and failed with my attempts to get anybody from TVam to contact me. Then I had a brainwave. In an act of desperation I wrote to Jimmy, who did his TV review chat around about the birthday announcements. He always came across as a decent guy with a heart and I admired his remarkable recovery following what he called his hiccup, He dealt with it with great honesty.

My daughter's birthday – March 9th 1986 – is such a good memory and funny. As he sat on the couch with Anne Diamond and Nick Owen he suddenly brought out the card from his back pocket, wished my Michelle a very happy seventh birthday and then went on to mention the birthday of his own granddaughter, Gemma. Anne Diamond abruptly told him to get on with what he was there for, talking about television. Cheeky Jimmy just raised his eyebrows and smiled. What a great character.'

UNBELIEVABLE, A MISS FROM THE PENALTY SPOT
DENNIS CHURCH, Ashford, Middlesex

'The first time I saw Jimmy play was during the 66/67 season. It was against West Ham at White Hart Lane. Greavsie that day both scored and missed a penalty. Jimmy missing a penalty was unthinkable. It just didn't happen. He was that good he just didn't miss.

Simply the greatest goalscorer I have ever seen. I was lucky enough to witness Jimmy's 200th and 300th League goals and to be one of the 36,622 to see him beat half the Leicester team before finally slipping the ball past future England keeper Peter Shilton. I would have to say Jimmy's best goal ever and I saw plenty. If only Sky Sports had been around in those days. I was lucky enough to meet the great man himself in 2009 and will never forget what a fantastic goalscorer and gentleman he is. The best ever and a true legend.'

GETTING STOKED UP WITH THE WIZARD

GEORGE BOSSONS, Newcastle-under-Lyme, now Cheshire

❛When I was a lad watching Spurs play my local team Stoke, our fans used to get nervous everytime he got the ball, and screamed in the hope it would put him off and stop him scoring. I remember running on to the pitch and shaking hands with Jimmy and our goalkeeper Gordon Banks, and saw it on Match of the Day.

Jimmy always says that one of his most memorable games was at Victoria Road. He partnered the Wizard of Dribble Sir Stanley Matthews in his farewell Testimonial Match when Stanley was 50 years old. Imagine, Matthews and Greaves together in the same forward line!❜

A COCKNEY KNEES UP WITH MOORO

GARY WRIGHT, Ilford

❛Spurs v West Ham around Easter 1969 ... Bobby Moore, Jimmy's great pal, fouled him by pulling him back when Spurs were on a breakaway attack. Jimmy ran straight for Moore and locked arms like in a Scottish reel and swung Moore around. Jimmy later called it 'a Cockney knees-up' and said he told Mooro he would meet him later in the Black Lion pub in Plaistow. Both Moore and Greaves laughed and the crowd roared with mutual merriment as the two great pals enjoyed the moment in a tense London derby. Sportsmanship yes but somehow it was more and the memory has never left me. Spurs won 1-0 and I think Jimmy scored but not certain. But that doesn't matter. It was the sportsmanship that mattered.❜

JIMMY PAYS THE PENALTY

TONY SADGROVE, Melbourne, Australia

❛I remember Jimmy missing a penalty during a 4-3 vicory over West Ham that was one of the most entertaining games I ever saw at White Hart Lane. In the same game Bobby Moore conceded a penalty when he punched the ball over the crossbar, much to the amusement of the crowd and players on both side. There was no automatic red card in those days. Today, he would have been off. Back then everybody laughed, which is an indication of how the game has changed.

Another outstanding memory is from the 1968 Leicester game when Jimmy and Allan 'Sniffer' Clarke had something of an upmanship battle. The game will always be remembered, of course, for Jimmy's magical goal, when he collected the ball and dribbled through almost the entire Leicester team before sliding the ball past goalkeeper Peter Shilton. Who said Greaves was just a goal poacher!❜

THE BEST IN HALF A CENTURY AND FUNNY WITH IT

TOM RIMMER, Southport

'Jimmy was simply the most natural goal scorer I have seen in more than fifty years of watching football. He is also probably one of the most humorous men to play the game at top level. The goal that sticks out in my memory above all others is when he ran from the halfway line through a Manchester United defence including the likes of Nobby Stiles, Pat Crerand and big Bill Foulkes to score a real beauty. It always featured in the Match of the Day opening titles until colour TV arrived in 1970.'

THE DAY JIMMY MADE ME SOB MY HEART OUT

DUNCAN FOSBRAEY, Sittingbourne, Kent

'I have many many childhood memories of the great man in action, but unfortunately the clearest memory of his wonderful career was one evening in 1970 when I was a 13 year old devoted Spurs fan, my bedroom a shrine to the team and Jimmy in particular. That evening my father came upstairs to my room and told me he'd just heard Spurs had sold Jimmy to West Ham and we had got Martin Peters in return. I can still feel the hurt now as I tried to hold back the tears (don't cry in front of Dad!!) and muttered something about how good Martin was and it was probably best for the team.

Dad went back downstairs and I just sobbed my little heart out! My hero for all those years had gone! I wanted to support West Ham but I couldn't, I wanted to like Martin Peters (he'd won the World Cup, he'd even scored a goal!!) but I hated him. I'd have to take down Jimmy's posters on my wall, I couldn't 'be Jimmy' in my garden again, dribbling around five Man U players and sliding it into the corner (how the hell was I meant to be Martin and 10 years ahead of my time - wtf did that mean??!!). I thought life had ended! Of course it hadn't but never since has the Lane had that collective, instinctive gasp of anticipation as it had when Jimmy got the ball at his feet facing goal......magic!'

THE ROAR OF THE LONG-DISTANCE CROWD

ANTHONY TONKING, Bedfordshire

'Back in1963 – having hardly missed a Spurs home match in five years – I elected to play parks football on Saturday afternoons. Our home pitch was at Tottenham Hale, a mile or so from White Hart Lane. When Spurs were at home we could tell when Jimmy Greaves had scored by the roar of the crowd. There was always an extra crescendo for a Greavsie goal, and we knew who had found the back of the net. We'd say: "Jim's scored ... again!"'

BOTH JIMMY AND I GOT STOPPED ON CUTS IN 1966
HENRY COOPER

'Whisper it, but I'm a Gooner. But that has not stopped me admiring Jimmy as one of the greatest footballers ever to pull on an England shirt. We have known each other since back in the 1950s when I was winning my first titles and Jimmy was making a name for himself with Chelsea.

He often saw me fight, and I often saw him play, particularly in the derby matches at Highbury and White Hart Lane and also, of course, for England.

I couldn't believe it when he was not picked by Alf Ramsey for the World Cup final. That was the year I challenged Muhammad Ali for the world heavyweight title at Highbury and got stopped on a cut. I suppose you could say Jimmy got stopped on a cut in the World Cup two months later.

As an Arsenal man I just wish he had joined us from AC Milan instead of that other lot up the road. I've always told him, 'Only one thing wrong with you, Jim ... wrong-colour shirt.'

WHEN GREAVSIE PUT GORDON BANKS ON THE SPOT

MARK ACKERMAN, Muswell Hill

'Spurs had a lousy away record in 1964-65, winning only one League game away –and that was against Nottingham Forest on Boxing Day. But in contrast they had a great home record that year, winning all but two matches and drawing those two against Leeds and Chelsea.

We always did well against Leicester so when they came to The Lane in April 1965, Spurs' fans were expecting a great result. And they got it as the Lilywhites swarmed to an overwhelming 6-2 victory and Jimmy Greaves got a hat trick.

One of his goals was a penalty which he took at the Paxton Road end. It was one of the funniest penalties ever witnessed at White Hart Lane, or anywhere else for that matter.

Gordon Banks was in goal for Leicester that day and he seemed to be trying to put Jimmy off by turning his back on him and fiddling with his gloves while Jimmy waited to take the kick (Gordon later said he was trying to dry his gloves on a patch of grass in the back of the net on what was a very muddy pitch).

Jimmy, as usual looking to do something different, rolled the ball into the other corner of the net while Gordon was still crouched over and unsighted. Much to his surprise and Gordon's anger the referee awarded a goal. As Jimmy and the Spurs (and some Leicester players) fell about laughing, Gordon was booked for protesting. Joker Jim had scored again!

All these years later, I still hold Jimmy up as the greatest goal scorer this country has ever produced.'

JIMMY, THE AUTOGRAPHS AND A JAG

PETER ASHTON, Kingston, Surrey

'I was too young to have seen Greavsie play at WHL, but as a treat my parents took me on a Friday afternoon of half-term to see Jimmy in an autograph signing session at a department store in High Wycombe called Murrays. He very patiently signed my photos of him taken from Christmas annuals and a bubblegum pack photo of him in the Chelsea kit that I had pasted in to my autograph book.

As we left the store someone pointed out a yellow Jag parked outside and said: "That's his car". I thought, "Cor, he must be doing well!" I still have the autograph book with his and Danny Blanchflower's signatures, two of the greatest players ever to pull on the Spurs shirt.'

TAKING GOALS TO NEWCASTLE

TIM ARMES, Swiss Cottage

'I have many memories of Jimmy Greaves but the one that always stands out is the goal against Newcastle, when Jimmy appeared to run most of the length of the pitch before scoring. The reason this remains in my memory is that Jimmy had been going through a bit of a "sticky patch" by his standards. It was towards the end of his wonderful career at Spurs.

From the moment he started to run with the ball it was as if the whole of White Hart Lane, including the opposition, sensed Jimmy was going to score one of his best goals – which he duly did. This sense of what he was about to do was palpable around the whole ground. The noise and the delight from the Spurs supporters was terrific, even though I was a boy at the time I can still recall the cheers and I still feel a tingle of excitement and pride whenever I think of that goal. Thank you Jimmy for such a wonderful memory.'

CORNERING THE FLYING PIG

TONY PHILPOTT, Essex

'As a 14/15 year old I was directly behind the goal, right against the wall, as Spurs were taking a corner against Liverpool at The Lane circa 1963/64. Jimmy was in the centre of the goal and, as the ball was coming in, curled in from the left by Jimmy Robertson, I distinctly heard Jimmy G. call, "Leave it Fatty"! The Liverpool goalie at the time was Tommy Lawrence, who was nicknamed the Flying Pig because of his heavy physique. Tommy duly obliged and the ball flew into the top right hand corner! I wonder what Lawrence had to say when he realised what cheeky Jimmy had done?

Jimmy truly followed the Danny Blanchflower code: "The game's about glory. It's about doing things in style, with a flourish. It's about going out and beating the other lot, not waiting for them to die of boredom."'

FACE TO FACE WITH THE GREAT ONE AT HIGHBURY

STEPHEN BOURNE, Mill Hill

'A few years ago I watched Spurs play Arsenal at Highbury in a friend's box at the Old Clock end. After the game as we waited for the crowds to clear I went out on to the terrace for some air and there, 20 yards away, was my hero Jimmy Greaves, who had been watching the game from another box. Just the two of us nodding hello to each other. I froze.

At nearly 50 years of age I was star struck and my biggest regret is not having the courage to go up to him and say thank you for the most wonderful football memories.

I would, in particular, have mentioned that goal against Leicester! I was standing on the half-way line at the front of the old East stand when Pat drop kicked the ball up field to the great man. He was standing just in front of me out on the right wing. He took the ball cleanly with his left foot and immediately began a weaving diagonal run across field towards the Leicester penalty area. He beat one then another and then another and another Leicester defender, leaving them trailing in his wake.

The anticipation in the crowd rose as it always did when Greavsie got the ball, the noise escalating as he neared the Leicester penalty area. He drew the keeper – a young Peter Shilton – and calmly slotted the ball home as if it was a training match.

The crowd went mad and amazingly we were still applauding this fantastic goal even after Leicester had kicked off to restart the game!

At this time in his career the great Jimmy was being talked about as a has been. His form had been patchy and he had been all but written off by the media. I remember very clearly the headline in, I think, the *People*, on the following day.

There was a picture across the back page showing three or four Leicester players on the floor revealing the Greaves route across the pitch with the headline: *"Who said he was finished?"*

Without doubt, my all time football hero. What on earth would he be worth today? A man who scored goals for fun with no fuss, just class. Thanks Jimmy.

ON THE ROAD WITH JIMMY AND Co
ALFRED GORDON, Gidea Park, Romford

Jimmy in my opinion was the greatest goal scorer of all time, and when my Dad took me to the Spurs matches from 1956 (I was 6 years old) to 1985 when he died I was lucky to see the double team and then the following year the same team but including Jimmy. The group of people we travelled with included Johnny " the Stick" and "One Armed" Lou, I am sure Jimmy will remember them as Johnny used to sleep in Jim's Football shirt as he loved him so much (note: Johnny was buried in the shirt!).

I was only 12-years-old at that time and Jim played football with me on the train with a bottle top. I was so lucky, as my dad knew so many of the players.

We often had dinner on the train back from an away game with the players, mostly with Les Allen and Terry Medwin. Cliff Jones and John White were always playing practical jokes on each other; for example, I remember Cliff pouring a full salt cellar into John's pocket.

My memories of Danny Blanchflower was him sitting alone in a compartment of the train reading a book, whilst next door there would be Bobby Smith, Dave Mackay and a few others playing cards. Great memories for me, and as I think back I realise how lucky I was to see close up a football genius like Jimmy Greaves.

A RATTLIN' GOOD TIME IN THE PAXTON ROAD STAND

KEVIN FIELD, Lincoln

'One of my favourite memories of Greavsie, which is also a family memory, occurred on March 9th 1967 when we played Liverpool in the fifth Round of the FA Cup. I went with my dad and for some reason my mum also wanted to come along. Unknown to me she brought with her an old wooden football rattle! She was born "Oop North" not far from Liverpool and therefore supported the opposition.

We were sat in the old Paxton Road stand with its wooden floorboards, which made a wonderful sound when being stamped by thousands of feet. Greavsie scored at our end to put us one up, and the stand rose to a man cheering and shouting. All that is except my mum, who sat there stony faced!

Before we had a chance to enjoy our lead, Tony Hateley equalised and my mum went mad. This time she seemed to be the only one in our stand on her feet, waving her rattle like a whirling dervish. I have never been so embarrassed. The match ended 1-1 and we lost the replay 2-1 after a retaken penalty.

When a Spurs striker starts to score on a regular basis, some say he is another Greavsie. This can never be, as there is only one Jimmy Greaves, the most naturally gifted striker British Football has ever seen, and we shall not see his like again.'

RESERVED AT THE COTTAGE

IAN PORTER, Weybridge, Surrey

'As a youngster I recall in the early sixties going to see Spurs reserves against Fulham reserves at Craven Cottage – Jimmy Greaves, England's greatest goalscorer, played for Spurs, and his pal Johnny Haynes – England captain and the master schemer – played for Fulham. Jimmy scored, of course. Both were recovering from injury. They did things like that in those days. The match was on a Saturday afternoon and attracted a crowd in the region of 10,000.'

CALL ME GREAVES, JIMMY GREAVES

DON HODGE, Neasden

'As a kid I wanted to change my name to my idol Jimmy Greaves and went through a phase when I would only answer to that name. A good few years later, whilst waiting in reception at what was then TVam, the great man himself walked past me, whereupon I pretended to faint in front of the receptionist. When she asked me what that was all about I mentioned the name-changing charade and, unbeknown to me, she mentioned it to Greavsie.

I asked her if she would kindly ask Jimmy to autograph one of my many Spurs books, and she said she would see what she could do. A few weeks later, again in reception, whilst waiting to go into a meeting, I received a tap on the shoulder, and on turning around there he stood, I nearly did bloody faint this time!

He said: "So you're the plonker who wanted to change his name then?" All I could do was splutter a few garbled sentences until Jimmy was called away, by Timmy Mallett of all people (I've hated him since then by the way! Mallett that is!).

Jimmy signed my book, not only on the inside cover but on all the photos of himself throughout the book. It has remained a prize possesion ever since. Happy seventies, Jimmy!'

WHEN THE G-MEN WERE G-G-GREAT TOGETHER
PETER HARRIS, Queensland

'I remember a gob-smacking goal against Manchester United in 1965 when Jimmy seemed to run from almost the half way line to beat a number of tackles on his way to scoring a brilliant individual goal.

I also, in a general way, remember the "G" men combination with Alan Gilzean where Jimmy used to be supplied by Gilzean's astute headed passes and neat knock-ons. I share my memories with my Dad now that we are both now down here in Australia. I get back to The Lane when I can, but I know that I will never see another like Jimmy Greaves.'

THE SIGHT AND SOUND OF A MASTER AT WORK
BOB REILLY, Ware, Herts

'I have so many memories of the wonderful contribution Jimmy gave to the cause of Tottenham Hotspur. I think, like a lot of fans the most outstanding one that comes to mind is the December day he made his first-team debut against Blackpool at White Hart Lane .

I can remember deciding to stand immediately behind the goal at the Park Lane end, something I had never done before as I always liked to stand higher up to be able to see the pattern of the play better. Needless to say my memory is of that spectacular first goal Jimmy scored in a Spurs shirt.

Dave Mackay took a long throw-in on the East Stand side, which was headed into the box by Terry Medwin and there was Jimmy who, with an unbelievable acrobatic twist of his body, threw himself backwards and all in one movement struck the ball with a powerful scissors kick into the back of the net.

I can still hear the sound of the ball hitting the back of the net. What a goal! I was so privileged to be standing so close to the action that day. Thanks Jimmy for all the wonderful memories. The day you left Spurs you took something with you that has never been replaced, though many have tried.'

'MR COOL' OF THE PENALTY AREA

FLYNN PREVOST, Epping

❛Jimmy Greaves was simply the reason I supported Tottenham. As a kid my dad would take me over to Spurs from our Essex home. I could barely see through those semi circular bars that sat on top of the wall behind the Paxton Road end and, like most kids I had a hero, and that hero was Jimmy Greaves. One particular match that sticks in the mind was a game against Newcastle at White Hart Lane. I think it was either 4-1 or 4-2 to Tottenham, but what I remember most were the two goals our Jim got. They were both at the Paxton end and right in front of me.

The first goal was side footed in to the nct from about 10 yards, not smashed into the net but placed into the smallest of gaps. It needed a cool, calm head to do it and that's exactly what Jim always had, even in crowded penalty areas.

The second goal was unbelievable. Jim received the ball near the half way line and went on one of those mazy runs like Lionel Messi does these days. He beat two or three players, leaving them all lying on the floor after they had failed to tackle him. Along with everybody else I was willing Jim to shoot as he neared the 18 yard box.

But what did we know? Instead he drew the goalie, pretended to shoot, rounded the goalie and calmly stroked the ball into the net … and the crowd went mad!

On the way home my dad and Icould not stop talking about it. Jim knew where the back of the net was, and there was no one better at finding it.❜

THE DAY JIMMY LEFT ME FEELING BEREAVED

HUGH DONOHOE, Bromley

❛I am a 50-year old fan and idolised Jimmy Greaves when I was a boy (still do of course). Jimmy was the man who scored the goals and I was Jimmy in the playground at school when we played football. But my most vivid memory was the evening I heard that Jimmy was to leave us for West Ham.

I cried my eyes out and was truly inconsolable. My mum didn't know what to do. In the next day or so, in an attempt to bring me out of my depression, she bought me a claret and blue scarf so I could be a West Ham fan and support Jimmy at his new club.

I wrestled with this possibility and wore the scarf for a bit. In the end the pull of Spurs was too much and the scarf was folded up and never saw the light of day again.

In a way Jimmy leaving Spurs was my first experience of a 'bereavement' and it taught me a lot. I have watched great players come back and be introduced to the crowd at White Hart Lane but the one I want to clap and cheer is Jimmy Greaves. The one and only and the reason I am a Spurs fan and also the reason I nearly left them.❜

HOW COULD EX-SPUR ALF LEAVE OUT OUR JIM?

COLIN ASHBY, France via Haslemere

'How excited I was when Jimmy first signed for Spurs from the mighty AC Milan in 1961. His first game and a hattrick against Blackpool announced his arrival. The way he could dribble and jink his way round defences was something perhaps only George Best has ever been able to repeat. The ball always seemed to be attached to his boots.

I loved watching him play for us and, of course, England. It was after our double that he joined and the pity was he did not win the League with us; he deserved that. He scored in the final that helped us win the FA Cup for the second year in succession, and who can forget the night he ran the Manchester United defence ragged, scoring three and it should have been four.

It is strange looking back. I don't like Chelsea, never had an opinion about them until Spurs playing them with Greaves being literally marked by Ron "Chopper" Harris, a man without any real talent other than to use and abuse the rules of the game in my opinion. He would live up to his name and reputation and set out to hurt Jimmy as early in the game as possible. Destroying his confidence and morale in the process. I hated him. *(note: Jimmy and Ron are best of mates these days!).*

As far as I was concerned Greaves was the man and he performed and did the business at international level as well. But then came our challenge for the '66 World Cup. Jimmy had not been at his peak fitness due to illness and had been struggling. He had not played in the build up to the finals. I remember distinctly the day of the final and the team was announced by Ramsey. Roger Hunt and Geoff Hurst up front and no Jimmy? I was gutted for our player. How dare an ex-Spur leave out the best goal scorer we had seen.

To me that put a dampener on the afternoon. Yes we won; after all that was what it was all about, but to see the forlorn figure of Jimmy at the end having missed out on what was the biggest day in footballing history, made me shed tears for him. How could Ramsey have left him out? If we had lost he would have been castigated by the press for his stubbornness.

I rejoiced in England winning the World Cup but Jimmy should have been there in the team, not watching from the stands with the rest of the non-playing squad members. He was better than anyone else and by not playing him the risk could have been too great.

How smug I felt the following season every time he scored to prove that he still had it. To miss out on a European Cup and the World Cup medal was and still is a travesty as far as I am concerned.

To me James Greaves was the maestro.'

A WELCOMING PREZZIE FROM TOMMY SMITH
RICKY TOMLINSON

'Greavsie, my arse! Doesn't it make you want to spit. All that talent as a footballer, then he comes into my game and proves he's a great stand-up comedian. Seriously, Jim, well done on hitting the seventy milestone. I've often shared thoughts and indigestion with you on the after-dinner circuit, and you know I rate you right up there with the best footballers I've ever clapped eyes on. But as a Scouser I've got to say that I'm glad Roger Hunt got his World Cup final medal. I loved it when Tommy Smith once gave you a prezzie before the kick-off of a Spurs match at Anfield ... the menu for Liverpool hospital!'

HANGING OUT WITH MY HERO GREAVSIE

BRIAN DENNIS, Whitstable, Kent

'The year was the unforgettable 1962 and Spurs had just won the FA Cup, with Greavsie scoring in the final against Burnley. Me, I was a kid of 15, born and bred in Northumberland Park N17. My mate's dad was the local Fire Chief and a Justice of the Peace, so he was summoned to do his civic duty at Tottenham Town Hall on the day the Cup was paraded.

We badgered him into sneaking us in and on the day we lined the staircase with the Mayor and other dignitaries, shaking the hands of all the players and Billy Nick! There we were on the balcony behind the players with thousands of fans including mates from school down below. Then the magic moment happened!

I was busting for a pee and went to the very plush toilets to do the business. I was standing there when all of a sudden I looked up to see Greavsie in the next urinal. He turned to me and winked. "All right son?" he said with that big, trademark grin. "What did you think of the final then, mate?" My mouth was still open, unable to utter a word and then he had zipped up and was gone, back to the party! Had I really had a close encounter with my all-time football hero or was it just a dream!

I have lived on that story for years now, telling it in a light hearted way to any one who would listen. Some 45 years later I attended with my son one of Greavsie's brilliant nostalgia nights and told my lad that I would approach Greavsie and remind him of our encounter – of course, he would be sure to remember it!

I was told in no uncertain terms that the least I could expect if I opened my gob was to be enrolled in the local home for the bewildered! So, yet again when Greavsie was signing my programme I stood open mouthed, unable to utter a word!

Fingers and toes crossed that after all this time I can forgive myself for the cowardice I have had to live with all my life!'

GREAVSIE IS BOOKED FOR LASTING FAME

KIMBERLEY CHAMBERS, Romford

'Unfortunately, I am too young to have ever seen Greavsie play in the flesh. However, like most Spurs fans, I am fully aware of JG's fantastic contribution to Tottenham Hotspur. Jimmy was without argument the best goal poacher ever to grace the pitch at White Hart Lane. The man is an absolute legend, and in the heart of every true Spurs fan, young and old, and he always will be.'

Note from Norman Giller: Kimberley – a dyed-in-the-blue-and-white Spurs fan – is challenging Martina Cole for the title of British Queen of crime novelists. When you've finished reading this book, make a date to read Kim. She's a Yiddette and worthy of your support. Her books are as exciting as a Greavsie goal.

WHEN THE CREW-CUT KID DESTROYED WOLVES
PAUL VIVEASH, Isleworth, Middlesex

'My abiding memory of Jimmy Greaves dates from September 1958, when I saw him in action for the first time. I was 15, living with my parents in Cambridge. I'd been to White Hart Lane a few times, and, with an Uncle who supported Chelsea, to Stamford Bridge on two or three occasions.

On this day, Chelsea were home to Wolves, the reigning champions. Greavsie, as I remember, wore a crew cut and his boots appeared to be held together by sticking plaster. That didn't stop him scoring five goals in a 6-2 victory. What impressed me was that – just 18 – he made England captain Billy Wright look like a parks player.

About a year after he joined Spurs, I moved to London and became a regular at White Hart Lane. You knew that if Greavsie was playing there would be goals, and he rarely let us down.

No-one will ever convince me that there has ever been a better goalscorer in post-war English football than the one and only, the great Jimmy Greaves.'

JIMMY'S HUNGER FOR GOALS
JOHN DUCKETT, Belfast

'My favourite Jimmy Greaves story is the one told by Terry Venables when he was a young pro at Chelsea. Jimmy arranged to give Terry a lift to the Bridge for a League game. Terry was waiting and waiting and waiting, when finally along came Greavsie in the Standard 8 that was his car at the time. Instead of driving to the ground, Jimmy diverted to a restaurant. This was only a couple of hours before the game, and Jimmy ploughed through a roast dinner and a dessert, while Terry nibbled at a salad. When they finally got to the ground, Jimmy showed no signs of having eaten a full meal and proceeded to bang in a hat-trick. Terry said that Greavsie was never ever conventional, and went against every rule in the coaching manual. But what a player, what a guy!'

WHEN JIMMY WAS CAUGHT SHORT
ALEX McGOLPIN, Cheshunt, Herts

'I have two unusual memories of Jimmy when Spurs were playing Liverpool in the mid-60's. In the first match he was through one on one with 'keeper Tommy Lawrence who came out and creamed him outside the box. Today he would have been sent off, but then we simply got a free kick and drew 0-0. The other time was an FA Cup tie against the Pool and we were 1-0 down and a great cross was put in from the right, but it was a fraction too high for Jimmy who was on his own in the middle of the goal and he put it over the bar. It was the only time I'd wished Jimmy was a couple of inches taller, because we ended up losing 1-0. The rest of my memories are all good!'

MY FIRST GIRLFRIEND'S SIGN OF THE TIMES

JOHN SIMPSON, Loughton

❛I was once given a small tab torn out of an old style autograph book by my first primary school girlfriend. It would have been around 1964 when I was nine. On the tab, so it seemed, was the autograph of my hero Jimmy Greaves. She had taken it out of her Chelsea-supporting elder brother's autograph book (without his knowledge probably) and given it to me. It was my first ever present from a girl. She knew how much I loved Jimmy.

Anyway, many years later when I was moving out of home and into the first house of my own I remember coming across it and thinking it was probably a forgery as it too clearly read Jimmy Greaves, when most people's signature bore no resemblance to their own name. Most looked just like scribble. I remember it had a little "o" over the "i" in Jimmy, rather than a dot. I smiled to myself realizing that Janet Hannan, as she was back then, and who I hadn't seen in years, must have forged it just for me.

Anyway I discarded it and thought no more of it ... until that was a few years later my mum and dad presented me with a copy of Jim's book *This One's On Me*. They said that they'd been up to Smiths in Ilford and Jimmy had been there signing copies, so they'd got him to sign one for me. And there staring up at me off the page was the self same signature that Janet Hannan had given to me all those years ago, replete with the little "o" over the "i". And I'd thrown it away!

Jimmy is the reason I support Spurs. He was my boyhood idol and still remains so even today aged 55. When I was looking for a team aged seven or so, Jimmy had just signed for Spurs and was scoring goals for fun. When I found out he'd spent his early boyhood years in Dagenham, which was where I lived, that was it. It was Spurs for me. I was one of very few Tottenham fans in what is heavy West Ham territory, but it didn't matter. Jimmy made up for all the abuse I used to get.

I loved his understated way of celebrating goals. No kissing, no diving head first into the corner flag area, no thrusting at the team badge. Just a wheel away from the goal and the raising of one arm with index finger pointing to the sky, chewing on his ever present gum. That after he had waltzed around the entire opposition defence.

I remember once being taken to see Spurs by my Dad who was from the North East and a Sunderland supporter. After the game he asked if everything was all right, as I must have seemed a bit withdrawn. I said, "Jimmy had a quiet game didn't he, Dad," to which he replied, "He scored a bloody hat trick, son!" Which indeed he had. I also recall Brian Clough once going on about his own goal scoring prowess and about how many goals he had scored in one particular season (albeit in the old Second Division playing for Boro'). He said: "And that's even more than bloody Greaves. And he was the best!"❜

A FAILED DRIVING TEST AND NOW THIS ...!

LOGAN HOLMES, Carrickfergus, Northern Ireland

'I started to support Spurs in 1964 and Jimmy Greaves with his goal scoring exploits became my instant hero. The goal he scored against Manchester United at White Hart Lane when he ran from the halfway line is one of many to be savoured.

I remember clearly the day in 1970 when the news broke that he had been transferred to West Ham United. In the morning I had failed my driving test but I wasn't too worried as I wasn't keen on driving. Later in the day I received news that my application for a university had been turned down – no problem as I didn't want to go there. However, later in the day when the news broke that Jimmy Greaves had been transferred to West Ham United, I was totally devastated.

Tottenham Hotspur without Jimmy Greaves was unthinkable. Who would take on Jimmy's goal scoring role? It would never be the same again without Jimmy Greaves in his white number 8 shirt prowling around the penalty area waiting to strike at the first opportunity of a goal scoring chance.

It took Spurs and me quite some time to fill the void left by the goal scoring exploits of James Peter Greaves whose record at Tottenham Hotspur will never be surpassed. Thanks for the memories, JPG.'

THE GENERATION GAME

IAN GRUBB, Langholm, Scotland

'I was far too young to see Jimmy play, but I am a third generation Tottenham supporter and my dad and grandfather were regulars at the Lane in the sixties. Both have assured me that he was a legend. Having seen clips and his goalscoring record, in my eyes he is the greatest striker to have played in England, if not the world.

So in my opinion and having listened to my dad and granddad Jimmy will always be a legend, and definetly one of the all time greats.'

BUMPING INTO A LEGEND

MARTYN BYRNE, High Wycombe

'I was working in an office just off Ludgate Hill, near Fleet Street in the early 80's. I was out getting lunch when I literally bumped into Greavsie. I apologised and then the penny dropped who it was.....OMG, it's Jimmy Greaves! I stood there like a total fool, gawping. He is to date the only person who has ever stopped me in my tracks like that. I should have congratulated him on his defensive blocking.

The reason I tell this story is that more than 20 years on it means a lot to me that I bumped into a Lane Legend. It just shows what the name Jimmy Greaves means in the Tottenham history books.'

WHY I TURNED DOWN THE HAMMERS
BARRY HENLEY, Kentish Town

'Jimmy Greaves in todays game would simply be priceless. To this day I have never seen another player who creates as much excitement as he did every time he touched the ball. When he had a chance, there was rarely any outcome other than a goal. Every shot was not only on-target, but placed neatly in the corner, often leaving the disheartened keeper rooted to the spot.

There was only one way to play him. Defenders, particularly Ron "Chopper" Harris, would come to the Lane with the sole intention of scything down Jimmy every time he made a move for the ball. But he usually got the better of them.

The only way I can put his popularity into perspective is by thinking back to when I was a promising footballer. West Ham offered me an apprenticeship, but I turned it down because it would have meant missing watching Jimmy play at the Lane.'

EVEN THE SCOUSERS LOVE HIM!
WILLIAM SMITH, The Wirral

'I was born in 1974 so I didn't have the pleasure of seeing Jimmy play in the flesh. However, I recall standing with my Dad on the old east stand (below The Shelf) and hearing many a mention in the early 80s about someone called Jimmy Greaves. One day after a match I asked Dad who he was and I recall him saying: "He was the greatest goalscorer Spurs have ever had". The statistics speak for themselves and Jimmy will probably always be the benchmark for any striker who plays for our club.

The first time I actually got to be in the presence of Jimmy was as recently as 2009. I have lived on the Wirral near Liverpool for several years and therefore have been exiled from many of my fellow Spurs fans. When a chance to see "An evening with Jimmy Greaves" came along I booked my tickets six months in advance.

The night arrived and as I approached the venue in my brand new gleaming Spurs shirt I was happy to see several other fans donning their colours amongst a couple of hundred locals. Shortly after we took our seats Jimmy arrived on the stage and I felt the same dizziness I felt when I met Steve Perryman (*Lane of Dreams* page 163) as a child. What pleased me most was the respect that the Scousers showed towards him. I have lived here for many years and have endured the "flash Cockney" or "Del boy" jibes, but for Jimmy they had nothing short of total admiration.

The first part of the evening Jimmy did a cracking stand up comedy routine which was absolutely side splitting. I consider myself to be a bit of a stand-up connoisseur and for my money Jimmy is up there with the best around. I wouldn't want to repeat any of his jokes as you most certainly need the comedy timing of a genius which he has in abundance. In the second half of the evening Jimmy was joined by his old pal

Ian St John and the great Roger Hunt, much to the delight of the Liverpool contingent. It was heartwarming to see such two great rivals as Jimmy and Roger obviously liking and respecting each other.

I expected Jimmy to take second stage to the two Anfield legends, but as the trio threw the floor open for questions a large man stood up and said in a thick Scouse accent, "Jimmy pal, can I ask if you'll come back and see us again?" to which Jimmy replied "Yeah if you want me to". The theatre then erupted with applause and loud cheers and Jimmy said "All right I'll come back soon". Jimmy Greaves in my experience is loved by Scousers and Spurs alike.

JIMMY CONTINUALLY GOT ME OUT OF MY SEAT

TERRY ENGLISH, Edmonton

I started to support Spurs when very young, watching through thick and thin when they were not a very good team. But it was all worthwhile when the glory, glory days arrived. What a team that won the double. Not many really household names, eg Baker, Henry and Dyson. The real stars were Danny Blanchflower, Johnny White, Bill Brown, Cliff Jones and the incomparable Dave Mackay. I dont think I missed a home game that season and saw every round of the F.A. Cup, culminating in the 2-0 win over Leicester in the Final.

You would not have thought it could get any better, but then Jimmy Greaves arrived. I was at White Hart Lane for his debut against Blackpool when he scored a hat-trick. Jimmy has given me more pleasure and got me out of my seat more often than any other player. You could absolutely guarantee that when he was one to one on the goalkeeper that he would score.

I vividly remember a 6th round cup tie away at West Brom, returning from a distant trip for a European midweek game. Jimmy was one to one on the goalkeeper. The action seemed to freeze while Jimmy waited for him to go one way and he went past him the other way to score. He seldom blasted a shot. His classic goal against Manchester United started Match of the Day for years, but he scored an even better goal against Newcastle (on film) but his best ever was against Leicester, when sadly there was not a camera in the ground to capture the magic moment.

My late Dad was a Spurs fan from the time he came down to London from Workington to find work. He regaled me and my brother with tales of the Spurs, especially the 1951 league title, but he agreed with me that Jimmy was the very best player to pull on a Spurs shirt. I often wonder just how many goals he would have scored had he played in the same team as Glenn Hoddle. I could go on for ever.

My father's devotion, passed to me, is now with the next generation. I have instilled my love of Spurs in my daughter Melanie and my son Andrew.

WHEN I TOLD GREAVSIE TO **** OFF!

PAUL RUSSEL, Abingdon, Oxfordshire

'I have a slightly different memory of the great Jimmy Greaves. He was doing one of his after dinner speaking events at Abingdon United Football Club and my brother Simon had a ticket for the evening but I had to work.

My mobile phone rang about 10.30 pm. It was some guy claiming to be Jimmy Greaves and saying that my brother had asked him to call to say hello (after a rubbish day at work I had forgotten the event was even on).

I said into the phone: "Yeah, right, of course ... I know it's you, Simon ... now f*** off," and I put the phone down.

It rang again. It was Simon who said you have just told Jimmy Greaves to f*** off!. Then Jimmy came on line again and was laughing as loud as my brother. I apologised and had a brief chat with him.

A couple of years later I had the chance to go to an Audience with Jimmy at which I never stopped laughing. What an entertainer. Jimmy Greaves. Top man.'

A GOAL FROM THE HALFWAY LINE

MARTIN AVIS, Isle of Wight

'I'm aged 59 now, and I've followed Spurs since my Dad took me to the Lane in 1956. I always knew of a certain Jimmy Greaves, the headlines at the time spoke of "the boy wonder" playing for Chelsea's U18's and scoring 114 goals in his last season in the juniors. What an unbelievable player he was (and I bet he still would be if he was in an over 70's team!)

When he came to Spurs in 1961 and scored a hat-trick on his debut against Blackpool, I thought all my Christmas's had come at once! In those days I used to go to all Spurs home games, and many of the away games too, so I have seen him score some very memorable goals.

However, I have to say that my all time favourite was against Man Utd, at the Lane, in 1965. We won 5-1, and Jimmy just destroyed them. He collected the ball just inside their half, speed and skill taking him past four Man U players, then the keeper to make the crowd go ecstatic. They used to show that goal on "Star Soccer" with Peter Lorenzo. I have so many copies of it, and I still watch it every now and then.

My son even drools over it. I have brought him up right and he, too, is a Spurs fan. I have a taped radio interview with Jimmy after he retired and Bill Grundy asked him what his favourite goal was. I sat forward in my chair expecting him to describe the goal against Man United, but he replied,"When I was playing Sunday league football, I shot and scored from the halfway line. Well, you know me, I didn't think I could kick the ball that far!" Classic Greavsie!'

I WAS JIMMY'S LAST FOOTBALLING PARTNER
FRANK BRUNO

❛Not many people know this, but I played alongside Jimmy in his very last appearance in a football match. It was in his son Danny's testimonial at Southend when Jimmy was about 50. Even at that age you could see that he was a brilliant footballer, and his fantastic record speaks for itself. We appeared many times together on television, and he sparred with me in a couple of programmes. Once, I remember, we had rehearsed a routine, but when it was live on TV I got out of rhythm with our sparring and made him wobble with a punch. He pulled me close and said, "Pull your punches, know what I mean Frank!" Jimmy is one of the funniest people I know, and I've rarely known anybody as widely loved as he is. It is a privilege to have him as a friend. ❜

JIMMY EQUALS FIVE ARCHIBALDS!

NICK HAWKINS, Bournemouth, Hotspur Magazine

'I never saw Greavsie play, as I was born only a few days before he moved to West Ham in a swap deal for Martin Peters. My Dad idolised him though, and when I started to take a keen interest in Spurs he told me that the Lilywhites once had in their ranks "the best goalscorer that ever played the game". "What? Better than Steve Archibald?' I asked. "Better than five Archibalds on the pitch at one time," Dad replied.

After hearing my father's words of wisdom as an 11-year-old boy, I made it my mission to find out more about the striker who was better than five Archibalds. I immediately took an interest in the old Spurs programmes that Dad left hanging around. I didn't let the lack of colour pictures put me off and took my time reading through his entire collection from the sixties, making notes on an exercise book of the games when Greaves scored. It must have taken me ages, as Tottenham Hotspur's number eight found the onion bag most weeks and usually more than once!

Not long after compiling my facts and figures on White Hart Lane's greatest striker, Santa delivered a video called 'The Jimmy Greaves Story'. I remember on the cover it proclaimed - 'The greatest goalscorer of them all!' I can hear Dad saying, "I told you so" as I hastily inserted the tape into the machine, eager to see Greavsie in action for the first time.

I was captivated from start to finish, as the late Brian Moore took me through Greavsie's career. I eventually wore the tape out, marvelling at Jimmy's mesmeric movements on the pitch and incredible eye for goal. Even as a young lad, I knew this man was a very special footballer. From then on, I was no longer 'Ardiles' or 'Hoddle' when kicking the ball in the park with my friends. I was now 'Greaves'.

I've been obsessed with football ever since, whether it's playing, watching, reading or writing about the game. Today, I work as a freelance football writer and contribute stories to the Spurs monthly magazine. And whenever I get writer's block, I take a look up to the poster on my office wall of my favourite footballer. It says 'Goals. Genius. Greatness. Greavsie.' Inspirational.'

Note from Norman Giller: Nick Hawkins is a bright young writer who is establishing himself as an authority on all things Tottenham Hotspur. His debut book has been written in harness with Morris 'Mr Spurs' Keston, and is justifiably called Superfan. *It is a riveting read about one man's devotion to a club (Spurs, of course). He has seen them play more than 3,000 times and has been closer to the players than any reporter or even club officials. He won their trust by always keeping their secrets. Read more about the book at www.visionsp.co.uk*

Jimmy Greaves says: *"Morris was like our 12th man. No matter where and when we played he was there. He was always there to help and advise if a player ever got into bother, and he knew more about what was going on at the club than any of us. But he never told tales out of school. He knew when to keep stum, and he won the trust of everybody at the club. Yes, a Superfan." Here's Morris on Jimmy ...*

A SUPER PLAYER PLEASES A SUPER FAN
MORRIS KESTON

•Jimmy Greaves is by some distance the best striker I've ever seen at the club. Some days you'd watch him and he'd do very little, but give him half a second and half a chance and the ball would be in the back of the net. He ruled supreme in one-on-one situations, displaying immaculate close control coupled with the poise and balance of a ballerina. I never tire of watching a goal he scored against Manchester United in 1965 on DVD. He received the ball 35 yards out with his back to the opposition's goal. He then turned on a sixpence before dancing past the converging tackles of Bill Foulkes, Nobby Stiles and Tony Dunne before drawing goalkeeper Pat Dunne and stroking the ball into the gaping net. Pure genius.•

A LEGEND AND JUST SUBLIME
JOHN McLEAN

•I first became a fan of Tottenham Hotspur way back in the 1960's at the age of about 10. Jimmy Greaves was my boyhood idol and he remains so today. He was, in my opinion, the greatest goal scorer of all time. He is a Tottenham legend. If I had to pick Jim's greatest goal it would have to be the one against Newcastle in 1969. I have just watched it again on DVD and it still makes me smile. Picks up the ball in his own half, sprints forward into the Newcastle half, beats a defender with ease, glides around the keeper and taps the ball into an empty net. Sublime!•

PUTTING A SMILE ON THE FACE OF FOOTBALL
LORRETTA FONTAINE. Tottenham

•When I think of Jimmy I think of his legendary catchphrase, 'Its a funny old game'. Who can possibly forget his memorable partnership with Ian St John, their presence on our screens every Saturday talking all things football, bringing joy and laughter to many. I am too young to have seen Jimmy play but history has informed me that Greavsie enjoyed a legendary career at the mighty Spurs and is one of the greatest players in our history. What a masterstroke by 'Sir' Bill Nicholson, who signed the legend that is Greavsie. How I wish I could have seen Jimmy play on the green, green grass of White Hart Lane, if only I'd born ten years earlier. Jimmy, I salute you Sir!•

LINKING LEGENDS BUCKLE AND GREAVES

MICHAEL MACKMAN, Tiptree, Essex

'My grandfather was Bobby Buckle, the first captain of Spurs. He died in 1959 and it always saddened me that he just missed out on the great Spurs era of the sixties. I was fortunate to be at college in London and watched Spurs – and especially Jimmy Greaves – on a regular basis in the late 1960's. Bobby Buckle's widow, my Grandmother, heard that I had been to a Spurs match soon after I moved to London and she wrote to me (basically telling me off for not writing to her and telling her about the match!) and asking what the Spurs ground was like now and how the team had played. This was the start of an ongoing correspondence over the next few years. She had no TV or radio, devoured newspaper reports of Spurs matches (but never took a Sunday paper) and I like to think my letters added something to her very active interest in the club. I was plied with questions in her letters about the players. Her natural tendency was to be formal – probably her Victorian upbringing, so she only ever referred to players by the proper name. Never a mention of Mike, Pat or Dave, but how tall was Mr England, how agile was Mr Jennings, if Mr Mackay was stocky.

Her great interest was, of course 'Mr Greaves'. She knew exactly how many goals he had scored and I can remember she wanted to know how fast he was. Apparently Bobby Buckle was very quick off the mark and she knew how important that could be, especially for a goal scorer. She told me that she remembered 'Bobby' describing play as 'pretty' and I think that was a very good description of a lot of the football I watched at Spurs in those days.

And so to the most memorable moments. I remember the cheeky free kick against Liverpool, the missed penalty, numerous apparent 'tap ins' (didn't he pick up some virus from hanging around in the goal area for too long one season?), bit I suspect like many others it is 'that' goal in 1968 against Leicester, with a certain Peter Shilton in goal. The thing I remember most about it was firstly the almost totally solo effort, which I have never seen before or since at that level of football, and secondly the fact that he received a standing ovation every time he went near to another part of the crowd. I have never seen anything like that before or since and I think it illustrated that those who were there knew that they had seen something extraordinary.

I have the photograph from the *Sunday Express* taken from behind the goal and the first player was only just getting to his feet when the ball was in the net. I sent a copy of this to my Grandmother, (making sure the word 'Sunday' didn't appear on it anywhere) with a fulsome description of the goal and the crowd's reaction to it. She was completely fascinated by the photo and we spoke at length about it when we next met. I remember her asking whether I thought 'Mr Greaves' was a 'good Spur'. I said yes, but I now think he was probably the best Spur ever.'

A DOWN TO EARTH HERO
MAUREEN TURNER, Chingford

'My memories of Jimmy Greaves are mainly from my older brother, Bill Bryant, who was always saying how brilliant he had played every match that he went to watch. I have one memory of him long after he stopped playing. About 12 years ago, my son was playing for Waltham Abbey Youth and they played a charity match at Grays. Jimmy was there and he was so friendly to all of the boys. He laughed and joked the whole time and spoke to everybody. He is such a lovely down to earth man.'

WE CALLED HIM THE GOAL HANGER
ROY CARPENTER, Walthamstow

'I have never forgotten the first time Jim played for Spurs. I was standing behind the goal at the Paxton Road end. Following a Dave Mackay throw, the ball came to him on the edge of the box at shoulder height. In a flash he was in the air, volleying the ball into the corner of the net. All these years later it remains one of the greatest goals I have seen and scored by the greatest striker of all time. He had such quick feet, and needed only a half a chance and the ball was in the net. We used to call him 'Goal Hanger Greavsie.' He scored so many memorable goals that remain truly unforgettable. The man was a genius.'

TWO LITTLE BOYS AND A MASTER AT WORK
MAUREEN CARPENTER, Hayle, Cornwall

'Jim had natural talent, a genius with a footballing brain; a true master of the pitch. My hubby Alan says his earliest memory was the fabulous hat-trick he scored against Blackpool in his debut. Alan has been a Spurs fan for more than 50 years and still rates him the best striker they have ever had.

My personal memories are of when they opened the gates at half time in those Glory-Glory days of the 1960s. I used to wheel my pram in with my two little boys, Ricky and Gary, so they could watch the legend. They were just toddlers but used to yell out, "Jimmy! Jimmy!"'

NO COMPLAINTS, HE JUST GOT ON WITH THE JOB
PETER SPRING, Chelmsford

'I loved Jim's ability to raise the spirits of the team and the fans. There was no one sharper than him in the box and he was a joy to watch. I dont remember seeing him ever complain to a referee in an era when defenders were vicious against him. He just got on with the job, and when he scored he made no great fuss and just trotted back to the halfway line, job done. An absolutely amazing player.'

YOU COULDN'T TAKE YOUR EYES OFF HIM

RANDALL NORTHAM, Cheltenham
(A REAL publisher. See his incredible book list at www.sportsbooks.ltd.uk)

❛I was there right at the start of Jimmy's Tottenham career, a fan in the crowd when he played for Spurs reserves against Plymouth. He was marked out of the game by John 'Cardiff' Williams, who allowed him just two kicks. Trouble was he scored with each one of them. Jimmy just strolled through the game, but you couldn't take your eyes off him.

When I was a reporter on the *Birmingham Post* in the early 1970s, Ron Greenwood disciplined five players following the Blackpool nightclub drinking affair. I was talking to Wolves manager Bill McGarry on the phone when the news broke and he offered to guess the names of the players .. he straightaway reeled off the correct names, with Jimmy and Bobby Moore first on his list. It was well known in football circles that they liked to bend their elbows. Everybody in the game admired the way he had the character to beat his problem.❜

The final word of the fans goes to life-long Spurs supporter Barry Hatcher, a renowned jazz records producer who has always considered Jimmy a footballer with rhythm, swing and style ...

THANKS FOR THE MEMORIES AND THE SMILES, JIMMY

BARRY HATCHER, West Byfleet

❛My first memory of Jimmy was back in August 1957. Spurs were at home to Chelsea for the first game of the 1957/58 season and he was making his debut for the Blues. The result was 1-1 and, of course, Jimmy scored, as he did when making his debut for all of the teams for which he played.

Being a Spurs season ticket holder I often didn't have an opportunity to go to away matches so would go and see some of my favourite players who were gracing other clubs. In 1958 my dad and I went to Stamford Bridge to see Chelsea against Wolves, and to have a look again at Jimmy. The result was 6-2 to Chelsea with Jimmy scoring five! This was stunning, especially as he was up against Billy Wright to whom he was giving five yards start and leaving him in his slipstream - Jimmy had really arrived and I was wishing he played for the Spurs!

By the 1960-61 season he was an established England international player, and in April 1961 I was privileged to be at Wembley to see England play the Scots. England were fantastic, winning 9-3 with Jim scoring a hat-trick and a certain Bobby Smith notching two goals. This was without doubt the greatest performance I ever witnessed by an England team, better even than the 1966 World Cup winning side.

I just couldn't believe that Bill Nick, having just won the double, was going to buy Jimmy but he did for £99,999. He made his first team debut on December 16th against Blackpool at White Hart Lane which Spurs won 5-2 with Jimmy scoring a blinding hat-trick, with one of the goals coming from a spectacular scissors kick.

Later that season Spurs faced Benfica in the European Cup at White Hart Lane which Spurs won 2-1 but lost 4-3 on aggregate. Greavsie scored a goal that was wrongly ruled offside. Spurs dominated the match and should have won but for some poor decisions from the referee. (Nothing changes). However, Spurs did win the FA Cup, beating Burnley 3-1 at Wembley with Greavsie scoring (of course).

The following season Spurs won the European Cup Winners Cup beating Atletico Madrid 5-1 with the man scoring two goals. This magnificent win was done without the services of Dave Mackay who couldn't play because of injury.

Over the next six seasons or so Jimmy scored a hatful of goals for both Spurs and England, gathering some unforgettable goals. Come March 1970 and something happened which I never expected – Spurs transferred Jimmy to West Ham in part exchange for Martin Peters. I was broken hearted as I truly thought Jimmy would end his career at the Spurs. Ironically, at the very start of the next season, Spurs played West Ham at home in a League match and I think the result was a 2-2 draw and, of course, Jimmy scored for the Hammers.

This was the first match of the season and I was disillusioned as to what was going on at Tottenham and I did not wish to watch the Spurs without Jimmy. So my dad and I decided to sell our season tickets to the person who sat next to us, and that was the last time I saw Jimmy play except in his testimonial match at White Hart Lane against Feyenoord, which Spurs won 2-1 and, fittingly, Jimmy scored.

What made Jimmy my favourite player of all time was that he went on to the pitch to entertain and was never interested in kicking or hurting an opponent. He played the game with humour and style and with the unique talent of scoring more goals than anyone else. I have been lucky to have had breakfast with Jimmy at the Camden Lock TV studios in the early eighties. Jim was working on a breakfast programme in those days and a dear friend (Maurice Kinn) asked me what I would like as a birthday present. As a joke, I said 'breakfast with Jimmy Greaves' and lo and behold Maurice pulled it off. Meeting him was one of the great moments in my life.

So, Jimmy, you've now reached seventy! Well I reached this milestone three years ago, and apart from waking up every morning with a different ache, it's not so bad. I can't thank you enough for the goals, skill, entertainment and fun you provided for the supporters of Chelsea, AC Milan, Spurs and West Ham and, of course, England.

Jimmy, I wish you a wonderful rest of your life, Enjoy each day, and on behalf of all of us lucky to have seen you play thanks for the memories. **9**

Extra-time: The Greavsie Numbers Game

JIMMY never bothered counting his goals. He left that to others. "I was too busy scoring them to count them," he says with that trademark cheeky smile of his. Sports statistician **Michael Giller** has been doing some adding up while playing the Greavsie numbers game. These were the goals that counted ...

357 goals in the First Division, an all-time record that will never be beaten because the division no longer exists (and don't forget he was being kicked and hacked by the likes of Chopper Harris, Norman Bites Yer Legs Hunter, Nobby 'The Toothless Tiger' Stiles and Tommy 'The Anfield Iron' Smith, none of whom would last one minute in today's gentle, sanitized game).

44 goals in 57 England matches, just five behind the all-time record of Bobby Charlton in 106 appearances.

SIX TIMES First Division leading marksman, another record.

SEVEN First Division hat-tricks, **SIX** hat-tricks for England.

124 League goals for Chelsea (1957-610), then a club record.

220 League goals for Tottenham (1961-70), still a club record.

13 goals for West Ham (1970-71), **9** goals for AC Milan (1961)

Illustration: Art Turner

35 goals in the FA Cup, and top scorer for his club in **12** of the 14 seasons in which he played in the First Division. **266 goals** in 379 Tottenham matches

491 goals in all matches at the time of his retirement from League football *in 1971 at the all-too early age of 31, and not counting the dozens of goals he scored in non-League football.*

Jimmy's most prolific goal-scoring season was with Chelsea in 1956-57, while still an apprentice professional. He scored 114 goals and Chelsea presented him with an illuminated address to mark the feat. On the first day of the following season he made his League debut and scored for Chelsea against Spurs at White Hart Lane. It was the start of the great goal rush.

Banks of England (with Gordon Banks) **Footballing Fifties**
The Glory and the Grief (with George Graham) **Banks v Pelé** (with Terry Baker)
Football And All That (an irreverent history of the game)
The Seventies Revisited (with Kevin Keegan) **The Lane of Dreams**
The Final Score (with Brian Moore) **ABC of Soccer Sense** (Tommy Docherty)
Billy Wright, A Hero for All Seasons (official biography)
The Rat Race (with Tommy Docherty) **Denis Compton** (The Untold Stories)
McFootball, the Scottish Heroes of the English Game
The Book of Rugby Lists (with Gareth Edwards)
The Book of Tennis Lists (with John Newcombe)
The Book of Golf Lists   **TV Quiz Trivia**   **Sports Quiz Trivia**
Know What I Mean (with Frank Bruno) **Eye of the Tiger** (with Frank Bruno)
From Zero to Hero (with Frank Bruno)   **The Judge Book of Sports Answers**
Watt's My Name (with Jim Watt)   **My Most Memorable Fights** (with Henry Cooper)
How to Box (with Henry Cooper) **Henry Cooper's 100 Greatest Boxers**
Mike Tyson Biography   **Mike Tyson, the Release of Power** (Reg Gutteridge)
Crown of Thorns, the World Heavyweight Championship (with Neil Duncanson)
Fighting for Peace (Barry McGuigan biography, with Peter Batt)
World's Greatest Cricket Matches **World's Greatest Football Matches**
Golden Heroes (with Dennis Signy) **The Judge** (1,001 arguments settled)
The Great Football IQ Quiz Book (The Judge of *The Sun*)
The Marathon Kings **The Golden Milers** (with Sir Roger Bannister)
Olympic Heroes (with Brendan Foster)
Olympics Handbook 1980   **Olympics Handbook 1984**
Book of Cricket Lists (Tom Graveney) **Top Ten Cricket Book** (Tom Graveney)
Cricket Heroes (Eric Morecambe) **Big Fight Quiz Book** **TVIQ Puzzle Book**
Lucky the Fox (with Barbara Wright) **Gloria Hunniford's TV Challenge**
Comedy novels: **Carry On Doctor** **Carry On England** **Carry On Loving**
Carry On Up the Khyber **Carry On Abroad** **Carry On Henry**
A Stolen Life (novel) **Mike Baldwin: Mr Heartbreak** (novel)   **Hitler's Final Victim** (novel)
Affairs (novel) **The Bung** (novel)
Books in collaboration with **RICKY TOMLINSON**
Football My Arse **Celebrities My Arse** **Cheers My Arse**
Reading My Arse (The Search for the Rock Island Line)
PLUS books in collaboration with **JIMMY GREAVES**:
This One's On Me **The Final** (novel) **The Ball Game** (novel)
The Boss (novel) **The Second Half** (novel)
Let's Be Honest (with Reg Gutteridge) **Greavsie's Heroes and Entertainers**
World Cup History **GOALS!** **Stop the Game, I Want to Get On**
The Book of Football Lists **Taking Sides** **Funny Old Games** (with The Saint)
Sports Quiz Challenge **Sports Quiz Challenge 2**
It's A Funny Old Life   **Saint & Greavsie's World Cup Special**
The Sixties Revisited   **Don't Shoot the Manager**
OTHER BOOKS BY TERRY BAKER
Jimmy Greaves At 65   **The World Cup 40th Anniversary Tribute**   **Banks v. Pelé**